GERMANY, AUSTRIA AND SWITZERLAND
IN YOUR POCKET

GERMANY, AUSTRIA AND SWITZERLAND
IN YOUR POCKET

A STEP-BY-STEP GUIDE
AND TRAVEL ITINERARY

BY RICK STEVES

Horizon Books

British Library Cataloguing in Publication Data

Steves, Rick, *1955 –*
    Germany, Austria and Switzerland in your pocket: a step-by-step
    guide and travel itinerary — (Pocket travellers)
    1. West Germany — Visitors' guides
    2. Austria — Visitors' guides 3. Switzerland — Visitors' guides
    914.3'0478

    ISBN 1-85461-035-X

© Copyright 1987 by Rick Steves
UK edition © copyright 1989 by Horizon Books
Maps Dave Hoerlein

This edition first published in 1989 by Horizon Books Ltd, Harper &
Row House, Estover Road, Plymouth PL6 7PZ, United Kingdom. Tel:
Plymouth (0752) 705251. Telex: 45635. Fax: (0752) 777603.

Typeset by TND Serif, Hadleigh, Ipswich.

Printed in Great Britain by BPCC Wheatons Ltd, Exeter

CONTENTS

Europe

HOW TO USE THIS BOOK

This book is the tour guide in your pocket. It lets you be the boss by giving you the best itinerary in Germany, Switzerland and Austria and a suggested way to use the time most efficiently.

Germany, Austria and Switzerland In Your Pocket is for do-it-yourselfers who would like the organisation and smoothness of a tour without the straight-jacket. It's almost having your strudel and eating it too. Since most large organised tours work to keep their masses ignorant while visiting many of the same places we'll cover, this book is handy for anyone taking a typical big coach tour—but wanting also to maintain some independence and flexibility.

This plan is maximum thrills per mile, minute and pound. It's designed for travel by hire car, but is adaptable for train (see train chapter later). The pace is fast but not hectic. It's designed for the visitor with limited time who wants to see everthing but who doesn't want the 'if it's Tuesday this must be Salzburg' craziness. The plan includes the predictable 'required' biggies (Rhine castles, Mozart's house and the Vienna Opera) with a good dose of 'back door' intimacy—cosy Danube villages, thrilling mountain luge rides, Swiss chocolate factories, a Black Forest mineral spa and traffic-free Swiss Alp towns—mixed in.

Germany, Austria and Switzerland in Your Pocket is balanced and streamlined, avoiding typical tourist burn-out by including only the most exciting castles and churches. I've been very selective. For example, we won't visit both the Matterhorn and the Jungfrau—just the best of the two. The 'best', of course, is only my opinion. But after ten busy years of travel writing, lecturing and tour guiding, I've developed a sixth sense of what tickles the traveller's fancy. I love this itinerary. I get excited just thinking about it.

Of course, connect-the-dots travel isn't perfect, just as painting-by-numbers isn't good art. But this book is your friendly Franconian, your German in a jam, your handbook. It's your well-thought-out and tested itinerary. I've done it—and refined it—many times on my own and with groups. Use it, take advantage of it, but don't let it rule you.

Read this book before you begin your trip. Use it as a rack to hang more ideas on. As you plan, study, travel and talk to people, you'll fill this book with notes. It's your tool. The book is completely modular and is adaptable to any trip. You'll find 22 tours, each built with the same sections:

1. **Introductory overview** for the tour.

2. **Suggested schedule** recommended for that tour.
3. List of the most important **Sightseeing highlights** (rated:
   ●●● Don't miss; ●● Try hard to see; ● Worthwhile if you
   can make it).
4. **Transport** tips and instructions.
5. **Food** and **Accommodation:** How and where to find the best
   budget places, including addresses, phone numbers, and my
   favourites.
6. **Orientation** and easy-to-read **maps** locating all recommended
   places.
7. **Helpful hints** on shopping, transport, day-to-day chores.
8. **Itinerary options** for those with more or less than the
   suggested time, or with particular interests. This itinerary is
   flexible!

The maps point out all the major landmarks, streets, and
accommodation mentioned in the book and indicate the best city
entry and exits for our plan. They are clear, concise and readable,
but are designed only to orientate you and direct you until you
pick up something better at the tourist information office. To get
the most out of the maps, learn these symbols:

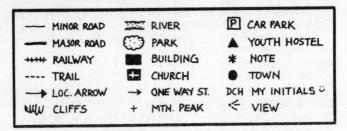

At the end of the books are special chapters on post-tour
options, tips on telephoning, eating and sleeping, speaking
German, driving, train travel, etc.

Travel smart

This itinerary assumes you are a well-organised traveller who lays
departure groundwork upon arrival in a town, reads a day ahead
in this book, uses the local tourist info offices, and enjoys the
hospitality of the Germanic people. Ask questions. Most locals are
eager to point you in their idea of the right direction. Use the
telephone, wear a moneybelt, use a small pocket notebook to
organise your thoughts and make simplicity a virtue. If you insist
on being confused, your trip will be a mess. Those who expect to
travel smart, do.

Cost

This trip's cost breaks down like this: A three-week car hire (split between two people, including tax, insurance, and petrol) or three weeks of rail and bus travel about £210 ($370). For room and board allow £20 ($35) a day, double occupancy £440 ($770). This is more than feasible. Add a couple of hundred pounds for fun money and you've got yourself a great European adventure for under £900 ($1,600) plus the cost of getting first to Frankfurt.

When to go

July and August are peak season—best weather and the busiest schedule of tourist fun, but very crowded, most difficult, and more expensive. Most of us travel during this period, so this book tackles peak season problems, especially that of finding a room. Early arrivals, calling ahead, and utilising local information sources are some of the remedies I'll discuss.

'Shoulder season' travel (May, early June, September and early October) is ideal. Try to plan a shoulder season trip for: minimal crowds, decent weather, sights and tourist fun spots still open, and the joy of being able just to grab a room almost whenever and wherever you like.

Winter travellers find absolutely no crowds but many sights and places of accommodation are closed or run on a limited schedule. The weather can be cold and dreary and night-time will draw the curtains on your sightseeing well before dinner time. The weather is predictably unpredictable.

Prices & times

I've priced things in local currencies throughout the book, with approximate sterling equivalents in brackets based on exchange rates as follows: £1 = 3.15 German marks (DM), 22.1 Austrian schillings (AS), 2.65 Swiss francs (SF). As a rough guide, 1 DM = 32p; 1 AS = 5p; 1 SF = 38p.

I haven't cluttered this book with many minor prices (e.g. specific admission fees and student discounts etc.). Small charges of less than a pound shouldn't affect your sightseeing decisions.

Prices as well as hours, telephone numbers, and so on are accurate as of the time of writing. Things are always changing and I've tossed timidity out of the window knowing you'll understand that this book, like any guidebook, starts to yellow before it's even printed. These countries are more stable than most European countries, but do what you can to double-check prices, hours and times when you arrive.

I have used the 24 hour clock (or 'military' time) throughout this book. After noon, instead of pm times, you'll see 13:00, 14:00 and so on. (Just add the 'normal' pm hour to 12). Sooner or later you'll need to get comfortable with this standard European time system.

The hours listed are for peak season. Many places close an hour earlier in off season. Some are open only on weekends or are closed entirely in the winter. Confirm your sightseeing plans locally—especially when travelling between October and May.

Borders, passports, visas and vaccinations

Travelling throughout this region requires only a visitor's passport at most. No vaccinations and no visas. Border crossings between Germany, Switzerland and Austria are extremely easy. Sometimes you won't even have to stop—just wave your passport at the guards as you roll through. When you change countries, however, you do change money, postage stamps, and much more.

You'll be dealing with great cultural diversity. Work to adapt. The cultural stew of Europe is wonderfully complex. We just assume Germany is 'Germany'; but Germany is 'Tedesco' to the Italians, 'Allemagne' to the French, and 'Deutschland' to the people who live there. While we think shower curtains are logical, many countries just cover the toilet paper and let the rest of the room shower with you. Europeans give their 'ones' an upswing and cross their 'sevens'. If you don't adapt, your 'seven' will be mistaken for a sloppy 'one' and you'll miss your train.

Keeping up with the news (if you must)

British newspapers are widely available on the Continent, though some editions may be a day late. To keep in touch with world news while travelling in Europe, read the *International Herald Tribune* which comes out almost daily via satellite from many places in Europe. However, news in English will only be sold where there's enough demand—in big cities and tourist centres. If you are concerned about how some event might affect your safety contact the consulate or embassy in the nearest big city for advice.

Being a tourist

We travel to Europe to experience something different—to become temporary locals. Tourists have a knack of thinking certain truths to be God-given and self-evident because they are used to having things and doing things a certain way that to them is the 'right' way. One of the beauties of travel is the opportunity to see that there are logical, civil, and even better alternatives.

Europeans, in general, welcome travellers and tourists if they are prepared to adapt and 'meet them half way'—after all, we

provide a source of income for many people. There is a warmth
and friendliness throughout the Continent. A eagerness to go local
and an ability—when something's not to our liking—to change our
liking, makes sure we enjoy a full dose of this European
hospitality. Fit in. If the bed's too short, the real problem is
you're too long.

Scheduling

Your overall itinerary is a fun challenge. Read through this book
and note special days (festivals, colourful market days, closed days
for sights, etc.). Sundays have pros and cons as they do for
travellers everywhere (special events, limited hours, shops and
banks closed, limited public transport, no rush hours). Saturdays
are virtually weekdays. Popular places are even more popular on
weekends. Most sights are closed during one week day.

It's good to alternate intense and relaxed periods. Every trip
(and every traveller) needs at least a few slack days. I followed the
Biblical 'one in seven' idea...religiously...on my last trip.

To give you a little rootedness, I've minimised one night
stands. Two nights in a row, even with a hectic travel day before
and after, is less gruelling than changing accommodation daily.

The daily suggested schedules and optional plans take many
factors into account. I don't explain most of these but I hope you
take the schedules seriously.

Car hire

If you plan to drive, hire a car through your travel agent well
before departure. Car hire for this tour could be much cheaper if
booked before you leave. You'll want a weekly rate with
unlimited mileage. Plan to pick up the car at the Frankfurt
Airport and drop it off there at the end of your trip. Remember,
if you drop it early or keep it longer, you'll be credited or
charged at a fair, pro-rated price. Every major car hire agency has
a Frankfurt Airport office. See which is cheapest through your
agent.

I normally hire the smallest, least-expensive model (e.g. Ford
Fiesta). For the bigger, more roomy and powerful inexpensive car,
move up to the Ford 1.3–litre Escort or VW Polo category. For
peace of mind, splash out on the CDW (collision damage waiver)
insurance. Remember, mini-buses are a great budget way to go
for 5 to 9 people.

Car v. rail

While this tour is designed for car travel, a section in the back of
the book adapts it for train travel. With a few exceptions, trains
cover this entire itinerary wonderfully, though it could work out

somewhat more expensive. While a car gives you the ultimate in mobility and freedom, enables you to search for hotels more easily and carries your bags for you, the train zips you effortlessly from city to city dropping you normally in the centre and near the tourist office. Cars are great in the countryside but a worthless headache in places like Munich, Bern and Vienna. To go by car or train...that is the question. For this itinerary, however, I'd drive.

Recommended guidebooks

This small book is only your itinerary handbook. To enjoy and really appreciate this holiday, you'll also need a directory-type guidebook and some good maps. I know it hurts to spend extra money on books and maps, but when you consider the improvements they'll make to your holiday—not to mention the money they'll save you—not buying them would be perfectly 'penny-wise and pound foolish'. Here's my recommended guidebook strategy.

To consider buying before you leave

1. A general low-budget directory-type guidebook—that is, a fatter book than this one, listing a broader range of accommodation, restaurants, sights, etc. Which one you choose depends on your budget and style of travel. My favourite by far is *Let's Go: Europe,* written and thoroughly updated every year (new editions come out around January). *Let's Go* covers big cities, villages, the countryside, art, entertainment, budget room and board, transport, etc. It's written for students on a student's budget and even though I'm neither, I use it every year. If its youthful approach isn't yours, and you've got plenty of money, then try Arthur Frommer's guides to Germany, Switzerland and Austria.

2. A cultural and sightseeing guide—The tall green Michelin guides (Germany, Austria, and Switzerland) have nothing about room and board but everything else you'll ever need to know about the sights, customs and culture. They are excellent (especially for drivers) and available in Europe. A small German phrasebook and dictionary is also helpful.

3. *Europe Through the Back Door* (by Rick Steves) gives you the basic skills, the foundations which make this demanding plan possible. Chapters on: minimising jet lag, packing light, driving v. train travel, finding budget beds without reservations, changing money, theft, travel photography, long distance telephoning in Europe, traveller's toilet trauma, laundry, and itinerary strategies and techniques. The book also includes special articles on 38 exciting nooks and undiscovered European crannies which I call

'Back Doors'.

4. *Europe 101: History and Art for Travellers* (by Rick Steves and Gene Openshaw) tells you the story of these cultures in a practical, fun to read 360-page package. Ideal for those who want to be able to step into a Gothic cathedral and excitedly nudge their partner saying 'Isn't this a marvellous improvement over Romanesque!'

Maps to buy in Europe

Maps—Most bookstores, especially in touristed areas, have a good selection of maps. For this tour I picked up the Bundesrepublik Deutschland Auto Atlas (by RV Reise und Verkehrsverlag, 1:200,000 scale) for Germany and the Osterreich Strassen Atlas (also by RV R. and V., 1:300,000 scale) for Austria. Each of these atlases has a good coverage of the entire country with an extensive index and handy maps of all major cities. For Switzerland I got by with Michelin maps 216 and 217 (or Die General Karte maps 1 and 2) with 1:200,000 scale. Throughout the tour you'll be picking up free maps of cities and regions at local tourist offices.

Freedom

This book's goal is to free you, not chain you. Please defend your spontaneity like you would your mother. Use this book to sort this region's myriad sights into the most interesting, representative, diverse, and efficient period of travel. Use it to avoid time- and money-wasting mistakes, to get more intimate with Europe by travelling without a tour—as a temporary local person. And use it as a point of departure from which to shape *your* best possible travel experience. Only a real dullard would follow this entire plan exactly as I've laid it out.

Anyone who has read this far has what it takes intellectually to do this tour on their own. Be confident, militantly positive, relish the challenge and rewards of doing your own planning.

GERMANY, AUSTRIA AND SWITZERLAND

TOUR 1   Fly into Frankfurt, pick up your hire car and drive to the famous medieval fairytale town of Rothenburg for your first night.

TOUR 2   Spend all of today exploring Germany's best-preserved walled town. Walk the wall, visit the exquisite carved altar and the fascinating medieval crime and punishment museum, and enjoy Germany's best shopping town.

TOUR 3   Today we drive south, exploring the 'Romantic Road' through the picturesque villages, farmhouses and onion-domed churches deep into the medieval heartland of Bavaria, and finally crossing into Austria. After hiking up to the Ehrenburg ruined castle and screaming down a nearby ski slope in a special summer-only wheeled luge on a concrete slalom course we'll catch our breath for the evening in the Tyrolean town of Reutte, Austria.

TOUR 4 This is castle time and nearby, back in Germany, is 'Mad Ludwig's' Disney-type Neuschwanstein castle. After touring Europe's most spectacular castle, stop by the Wies church — a textbook example of Bavarian Rococo bursting with curly curlicues, and visit Germany's wood-carving capital, Oberammergau, to window shop and tour the great Passion Play Theatre. Fill the afternoon with more of King Ludwig's extravagances, this time in his more liveable Linderhof palace. Back in Reutte, slap dance and yodel with a Tyrolean Folk Evening.

TOUR 5   Dilly-dally through three hours of Bavarian beauty north to Munich. Spend the afternoon orienting yourself in the old centre of town with its colourful pedestrian arcade. Evenings are best spent in Munich's crazy beerhalls — great oom-pah music, rowdy Bavarian atmosphere, big beers, big pretzels, and no-nonsense buxom beer maids who pull mustard packets from their cleavages.

TOUR 6   Today is spent immersed in Munich's art and history—crown jewels, Baroque theatre, Wittelsbach palaces, great art, beautiful parks and gardens.

TOUR 7   And on the seventh day we'll rest—but only until noon when we take the autobahn south to Salzburg, visiting

Germany, Austria & Switzerland

Hitler's mountain hideaway, Berchtesgaden, on the way. We'll tour a fun salt mine putting on an old miner's outfit, riding the tiny train into the mountain to slide down long splinter-free bannisters, cruise subterranean lakes and learn about old-fashioned salt mining.

TOUR 8   After enjoying the sights and castle of Salzburg, leave Mozart's hometown for *Sound of Music* country. After a very scenic afternoon in the Salzkammergut Lake District (alive with the S.O.M.) check into a private home in the postcard-pretty fjord-cuddling town of Hallstatt.

TOUR 9   Take a short intermission from Austria's fairytales to make a pilgrimage to the powerful Mauthausen concentration camp. Then follow the Danube through its most romantic section, lined with ruined castles, glorious abbeys, vineyard upon vineyard, small towns, and on into Vienna.

TOUR 10   Vienna, the easternmost tip and most exciting historic and cultural city of this tour, was the Hapsburg capital. It excels in art, tombs, palaces, pastries, coffee shops, and music. In other words, you'll be very busy today.

TOUR 11   After another Vienna morning and the afternoon at

the Schonbrunn Palace, Versailles' eastern rival, take the autobahn
five hours west to Innsbruck, sleeping in a nearby village.

TOUR 12   After some Alpine joy-riding you'll cross into
Switzerland. Appenzell—traditional and cosy—is the best first taste
of Heidi Land. This is cowbell country, no staggering mountains
yet, just a chance to savour the small-town ambience of a country
whose cities have become quite sleek and modern.

TOUR 13   Today we visit the Ballenberg Open Air Folk
Museum. Countless historic buildings have been moved to this
huge park to give us tourists an intimate walk through every
corner of Switzerland's diverse culture. Thirty minutes away is
the grand old resort of Interlaken, and south of there, a gondola
will lift you high above the valley into the terrific traffic-free
Alpine village of Gimmelwald.

TOUR 14   Today we'll learn why they say 'if Heaven isn't what
it's cracked up to be send me back to Gimmelwald'. All day is
free to frolic and hike, high above the stress and clouds of the
real world. This is your holiday from your busy holiday.
Recharge your tourist batteries.

TOUR 15   After a morning walk, drive south to Lake Geneva to
tour the very romantic Chateau Chillon and enjoy a taste of
French-speaking Switzerland.

TOUR 16   For the highlights of French Switzerland, we'll tour
the resort towns and rugged wine road of Lake Geneva, the
spectacularly set hometown of Gruyere cheese, and a nearby
chocolate factory. We'll spend the evening in Murten—Switzerland's best preserved walled town.

TOUR 17   Today is for the Swiss capital—Bern. Stately but
human, classy but fun, Bern is the best look at urban
Switzerland. For dinner, drive into Germany's Black Forest to the
charming and overlooked village of Staufen.

TOUR 18   The Black Forest is filled with tourists and cuckoo
clocks. It's also swimming with soothing mineral spas, Germany's
healthiest air and sunniest climate, traditional villages and folk
fests and wonderful wooded drives. After a quick look at the city
of Freiburg, we'll enjoy a scenic drive through the heart of this
legendary forest, and find our hotel in Baden Baden. Today's
grand finale, a two hour 'Roman Irish' bath complete with
massage, will show you why this place was Europe's leading spa a

hundred years ago

TOUR 19 Today we drive to Roman Trier, Germany's oldest city, and explore the peaceful Mosel River from there to the pleasant village of Zell.

TOUR 20 Explore more of the sleepy Mosel, so much more relaxing than the busy and industrial Rhine. After touring Germany's most exciting medieval castle, Berg Eltz, we'll drive to Bonn.

TOUR 21 Today we break again from storybook Germany to sample two real no-nonsense cities. Bonn is West Germany's capital and a colourful modern university city. Koln, which, like most German cities, rose gleaming and muscular from the ashes of WWII, is a cheery modern city with Germany's finest Gothic cathedral and some excellent art.

TOUR 22 Our grand finale is a day of cruising the Rhine and climbing through its castles. We'll cruise from Koblenz to Mainz and tour Rheinfels castle above the town of St Goar.

When you return to Frankfurt the circle is complete and you've experienced the best Germany, Switzerland and Austria have to offer.

TOUR 1

GERMANY

95,000 square miles.
62 million people (about 650 per square mile, and declining slowly).
One deutschmark = 32p; £1 = 3.15 DM.

Ja, Deutschland. Energetic, efficient, organised, and Europe's economic muscleman. 85% of its people live in cities and average earnings are among the highest on earth. 97% of the workers get a one-month paid holiday, and during the other eleven months they create a gross national product of about one-third of the USA's. Germany has risen from the ashes of WWII to become the world's fifth biggest industrial power, ranking fourth in steel output and nuclear power, third in car production. It shines culturally, beating all but two countries in production of books, Nobel laureates and professors. And its bustling new cities are designed to make people feel happy to be there.

While northern Germany is Protestant and the populace assaults life aggressively, southern Germany is Catholic, more relaxed and leisurely. The southern German, or Bavarian, dialect is to High (northern) German what the dialect of Yorkshire is to the South East of England. This historic north–south division is less pronounced these days as Germany becomes a more and more mobile society.

Germany's most interesting tourist route today—Rhine, Romantic Road, Bavaria—was yesterday's most important trade route, where Germany's most prosperous and important medieval cities were located. Remember, Germany as a nation is just barely 100 years old. In 1850 there were 35 independent countries in what is now Germany. In medieval times there were over 300, each with its own weights, measures, coinage and king. Many were surrounded by what we would call iron curtains. This helps explain the many diverse customs found in such a compact land. The foreign image of Germany is Bavaria where the countryside is most traditional.

Practise your German energetically because all but two days of this tour are in German-speaking country. For bitte or wurst, you'll have to learn a little Deutsch.

Germans eat lunch from 12 noon to 3 pm and dinner between 6pm and 9pm. Each region has its own gastronomic twist, so order local house specials whenever possible. Fish and venison are good and don't miss the sauerkraut. Great beer and white wines

abound. Try the small local brands. 'Gummi Bears' are a local
gumdrop sweet with a cult following (beware of imitations—you
must see the word 'Gummi'), and Nutella is a chocolate nut
spread speciality that may change your life.

Banks are generally open 8am – 12:30 pm and 1:30 pm – 4 pm,
other offices from 8 am to 4 pm. August is a holiday month for
workers—but that doesn't really affect us tourists.

ARRIVE IN FRANKFURT

How much you do today depends on what time your flight
arrives. Try to arrive by midday so we can count on a couple of
hours of sightseeing along Germany's Romantic Road before
reaching Rothenburg (pron. *ROW*-ten-burg).

Suggested Schedule	
?	Arrive at Frankfurt airport. Pick up reserved car, hit the autobahn. If early, visit Wurzburg. Take Romantic Road from Bad Mergentheim to Rothenburg.
17:00	Check into Rothenburg hotel.
Evening	Free in Rothenburg.

Frankfurt's airport (Flughaven), just a 12-minute train ride from
the city centre (6 trips/hour, 3DM (£1)), is very efficient and
'user friendly'. It has everything an airport could need—showers
(£1.70), left-luggage office (75p/day), banks open 7:30 – 21:00 with
fair rates, a handy train station, a decent waiting lounge where
you can sleep overnight, easy hire car pick-up, plenty of parking,
and an information booth.

The most important chores upon arrival in Frankfurt are to call
your Rothenburg hotel to reserve or reconfirm your room, change
some money into deutschmarks, and leave. If you're driving, pick
up your car and follow the green autobahn signs for Wurzburg.

Train travellers can buy a ticket at the airport station where
they'll catch a train directly to Wurzburg and connect to
Rothenburg.

Sightseeing highlights between Frankfurt and Rothenburg
● ● **Wurzburg**—A historic city, though freshly rebuilt since
WWII, Wurzburg is worth a stop to see its impressive Prince
Bishop's Residenz and its bubbly Baroque chapel (Hofkirche).
This is a Franconian Versailles with grand stairways, 3-D art, and

a huge fresco by Tiepolo. Tag along with a tour if you can find
one in English or buy the fine little (60p) guidebook. Be sure to
take in the sculptured gardens. Open daily 9:00 – 17:00 April –
September (closed Mondays), and 10:00 – 15:30 October – March.
Last entry one-half hour before closing, admission 3.50 DM
(£1.10). Easy parking, short walk from station.

●●● **Romantic Road (Romantische Strasse)**—The best way
to connect Frankfurt and Munich or Fussen is via the popular
Romantic Road. This winds you past the most beautiful towns
and scenery of Germany's medieval heartland. Any tourist office
can give you a brochure listing the many interesting Baroque
palaces, lovely carved altarpieces, and walled medieval cities you'll
pass along the way.

From Wiesbaden, Frankfurt or Wurzburg in the north, to
Munich or Fussen in the south, the route includes these
highlights:

Wurzburg—Old town along Main River under Marienburg fortress. Outstanding Baroque Prince Bishop's Residenz and chapel
(details above).

Weikersheim—Palace with fine Baroque gardens (prime picnic
spot), folk museum and fine old square.

Herrgottskapelle—One mile from Creglingen, Tilman
Riemenschneider's greatest carved altarpiece in a peaceful church.
Fast and fun 'finger hut' (thimble) museum just across the street.
Both sights open till 18:00 and only 1 DM (32p).

Rothenburg o.d. Tauber—See tomorrow's plan.

Dinkelsbuhl—Rothenburg's little sister, pretty, beautifully
preserved walled town, with twenty towers and gates surrounding
it. 'Kinderzeche' children's festival turns this town wonderfully
on end each mid-July. Tourist info tel. 09851-3031.

Rottenbuch—Impressive church, nondescript village in lovely
setting.

Wieskirche—The best Baroque-Rococo church in Germany. In a
sweet meadow. Outstanding!

Neuschwanstein– Mad King Ludwig's Disney-esque castle,
described later.

The drive in general gives you a good look at rural Germany. My
favourite sections are from Weikersheim to Rothenburg and from
Landsberg to Fussen. By car, simply follow the green 'Romantische Strasse' signs.

By train...take the bus. The Europa Bus Company makes this
trip twice a day in each direction. The ride costs about £25 ($40).
Each bus has a guide who hands out brochures and narrates the
journey in English, with stops for about an hour in the towns of
Rothenburg and Dinkelsbuhl and quickly at a few other

attractions. There is no quicker or easier way to travel across Germany and get such a good dose of the countryside.

Bus reservations aren't necessary (except possibly on a summer weekend, call 069/7903240 three days in advance) and you can stop over where you like.

Frankfurt—Probably a nice place to live, but I wouldn't want to visit there. Don't visit Frankfurt unless your only alternative is killing time at the airport before flying home. If that happens, pick up a city map at the tourist information office (T.I.) in the station, walk down sleazy Kaiserstrasse past Goethe's house (a very mediocre sight) to Romerberg, Frankfurt's lively market square. A string of museums is just across the river along Schaumainkai (all open Tues–Sat, 10:00–17:00). Whatever you do, don't drive or sleep in Frankfurt.

Transport

The 2½ hour drive from the airport to Rothenburg is very straightforward. The airport is right on the Wurzburg highway. It's a 90 minute, 75-mile straight drive to Wurzburg. The 'Spessart' rest area about half-way there has a tourist info office with a friendly man who can telephone Rothenburg—and speak German for you.

Take the 'Wurzburg/Stuttgart/Ulm road 19' exist and follow 19 south to Bad Mergenheim where a very scenic slice of the Romantic Road will lead you right into Rothenburg. If you're plugging in a stop at Wurzburg, take the later 'Heidingsfeld-Wurzburg' exit and follow the signs to 'Stadtmitte', then to 'Residenz'. To leave Wurzburg, follow the Stuttgart/Ulm road 19 signs from the centre of town south.

Train travellers will have missed the Romantic Road bus on this first day of arrival so will have to go straight to Rothenburg with a possible stop in Wurzburg. (The Residenz is just a short walk from the station.) The train ride from the airport to Rothenburg goes airport–Frankfurt Central–Wurzburg–Steinach–Rothenburg with trains departing from the airport at 7:00, 9:00, 10:00, 11:00, 13:00, 15:00 and 16:00, from Frankfurt Central 21 minutes later, arriving in Wurzburg in about 2 hours and arriving in Rothenburg (after a change in Steinach) in approximately 3½ hours. The Romantic Road bus tour leaves from Europa bus stops next to the Frankfurt station (south side, 8:15 departure daily) and at the Wurzburg station (daily 9:00, never full).

Food and accommodation

Rothenburg is crowded with visitors (including what is probably

Europe's greatest single concentration of Japanese tourists), but
finding a room is no problem. From the main square (which has
a tourist office with room-finding service), just walk downhill on
Schmiedgasse until it becomes Spitalgasse. This street has plenty
of gasthauses, zimmers (£6 ($10) per person with breakfast)
and two fine £1.75 ($3)-a-night youth hostels (in German,
'Jugendherberge', tel. 09861-4510).

I stay in Spitalgasse 28 **Hotel Goldene Rose,** tel. 09861-4638,
for about £6.75 ($12) a night. Less expensive yet and very
friendly is a room in the home of **Herr Moser** on Spitalgasse 12
(tel. 5971). Also good is **Gasthaus Raidel** (Wenggasse 3, tel.
3115, 24 DM (£7.60) per person, will hold a room for a phone
call), **Pension Poschel** (Wenggasse 22, tel. 3430, 20 DM
(£6.35)), **Pension Becker** (Rosengasse 23, tel 5562, 22 DM (£7))
and the friendly zimmer of English-speaking **George and Frida
Ohr** (Untere Schmiedgasse 6 near the criminal museum, tel.
4966, 40 DM doubles (£12.75)).

For a peaceful night in a nearby village consider the clean,
quiet, and comfortable old **Gasthof Zum Schwarzen Lamm** in
the town of Detwang just below Rothenburg (50 DM doubles
(£16)). While they serve good food, the Eulestube is a local style
restaurant nearby full of happy campers. For more village
zimmers look in Detwang or in little Bettwar a bit further down
the road.

TOUR 2

ROTHENBURG OB DER TAUBER

Today we stay put, enjoying Europe's most exciting medieval town. Rothenburg is well worth two nights and a whole day. In the Middle Ages, when Frankfurt and Munich were just wide spots in the road, Rothenburg was Germany's second largest city with a whopping population of 6,000. Today it's her best-preserved medieval walled town, enjoying tremendous tourist popularity without losing its charm.

Suggested schedule	
7:00	Walk on wall.
8:30	Breakfast.
9:00	T.I. to confirm plans, walking tour? Climb tower, visit St Jacob's Church, tour Criminal Museum, buy picnic.
12:00	Picnic in castle garden, rest.
14:00	Shopping or walk through the countryside.
Evening:	Free in Rothenburg.

Too often Rothenburg brings out the shopper in visitors before they've had a chance to appreciate the historic city. True, this is a great place to do your German shopping, but first see the town. The T.I. on the market square has guided tours in English. If none are scheduled, hire a private guide. For about £15 ($25), a local historian—who's usually an intriguing character as well—will bring the ramparts alive. A thousand years of history are packed between the cobbles. Call Karen Bierstedt, tel. 09861–2217, or Manfred Baumann, tel. 4146.

First, pick up a map and information at the T.I. on the main square (open 9:00–18:00, on Sat 9:00–12:00, closed Sun). Confirm sightseeing plans and ask about the daily 13:30 walking tour and evening entertainment (tel. 40492).

To orientate yourself, think of the town map as a human head. Its nose (the castle) sticks out to the left, the neck is the lower panhandle part (with the youth hostels and my favourite hotel).

Sightseeing highlights

● **Walk the Wall**—1½ miles around, great views, good orientation. Can be done speedily in one hour, requires no special

sense of balance. Photographers will go through lots of film. Ideal
before breakfast or at sunset.

●● **Climb Town Hall Tower**—Best view of town and
surrounding countryside. Open 9:30–12:30, 13:00–17:00, 1 DM
(32p). Rigorous but interesting climb.

●● **Medieval Crime and Punishment Museum**—The best of
its kind, full of fascinating old legal bits and pieces, instruments
of punishment and torture, even a special cage—complete with a
metal gag—for nags. Exhibits in English. Open 9:30–19:00, 4
DM (£1.30).

●● **St Jacob's Church**—Here you'll find a glorious 500-year-
old Riemenschneider altarpiece located up the stairs and behind
the organ. Riemenschneider was the Michelangelo of German
woodcarvers. This is the one 'must see' art treasure in town.
Open daily 9:30–17:30, Sun 10:30–17:30, 2 DM (64p).

Meistertrunk Show, Main Square at 11:00, 12:00, 13:00, 14:00,
15:00, 21:00, or 22:00—For the ritual gathering of the tourists to
see the breathtaking re-enactment of the Meistertrunk story.
You'll learn about the town's most popular legend, a fun, if
fanciful, story. Hint: for the best show, don't watch the clock,
watch the open-mouthed tourists.

● **Walk in the countryside**—Just below the Burggarten (castle
garden) in the Tauber Valley is the pretty, skinny 600-year-old
castle/summer home of May Toppler (open 10:00–12:00 and
14:00–17:00). It's furnished intimately and is well worth a look.
Notice the photo of bombed out 1945 Rothenburg on the top
floor. Across from the castle a radiantly happy lady will show you
her 800-year-old water-powered flour mill called the Fuchsmuhle.
From here you can walk on past the covered bridge and huge
trout to the peaceful village of Detwang. Detwang is actually
older than Rothenburg, with another great Riemenschneider
altarpiece.

Swimming—Rothenburg has a great modern recreation centre
with an outdoor pool, a few minutes walk down the Dinkelsbuhl
Road, open 10:00–20:00, 2 DM (64p).

Franconian Open Air Museum—Twenty minutes drive from
Rothenburg in the undiscovered 'Rothenburgy' town of Bad
Windsheim is a small open air folk museum that, compared with
others in Europe, isn't much, but is trying very hard and gives
you the best look around at traditional rural Franconia.

Shopping

Rothenburg is one of Germany's best shopping towns. Make a
point to do your shopping here. Lovely prints, carvings, wine
glasses, Christmas tree ornaments and beer steins are very
popular. The 'Friese' shop (just west of the tourist office on the

corner across from the public w.c.) is friendly, good and gives shoppers with this book tremendous service: 10% discount, postage at cost, for items mailed, and a free Rothenburg map. Anneliese who runs the place with her kids, Jurgen and Berni, even changes money at the best rates in town with no extra charge. Hummel figurines, apparently, are sold at regulated prices throughout Germany.

For those who prefer to eat their souvenirs, the Backereis, with their succulent pastries, pies and cakes, are pleasantly distracting. Skip the good looking but bad tasting 'Rothenburger Schnee Balls'.

Evening fun and beer drinking

The best beer garden for summer evenings is just outside the wall at the Rodertor. Closer to home, enjoy good wine, fun accordian music and a surly waiter (21:00 except Tues and Sun) at Plonlein 4.

Itinerary options

This 'two nights and a full day' plan assumes you have a car. Those travelling by train taking the Romantic Road bus tour must leave around 13:30 so you'll have to decide between half a day or 1½ days here. For sightseeing, half a day is enough. For a rest a day and a half sounds better.

A popular pastime seems to be the search for 'little, untouristy Rothenburgs'. There are many (Michelstadt, Miltenberg, Bamberg, Bad Windsheim, Dinkelsbuhl, and others I decided to forget) but none holds a candle to the king of medieval German cuteness. Rothenburg is best even with crowds and over-priced souvenirs. Save time and mileage and be satisfied with the winner.

TOUR 3

ROMANTIC ROAD TO TYROL

Today we wind through Bavaria's Romantic Road, stopping
wherever the cows look friendly or a village fountain beckons.
After a glimpse of Europe's most fairy-tale castle, we'll cross into
Tyrolia in Austria to explore the desolate ruins of a medieval
castle and finish the day with an evening of slap dancing,
yodelling and local music.

Suggested schedule	
7:30	Breakfast.
8:30	Romantic Road, head for Austria.
9:30	Stop in Dinkelsbuhl, buy picnic.
10:00	Drive south on Romantic Road, picknicking en route to Austrian border.
14:00	Cross into Austria, check into Reutte hotel.
15:00	Walk to Ehrenburg ruins.
16:30	Luge ride down ski slope in a go-cart.
18:00	Rest and dinner.
20:30	Tyrolean folk evening.

Get an early start to enjoy the quaint hills and rolling villages of
what was long ago Germany's major medieval trade route. After a
quick stop in Dinkelsbuhl, cross the baby Danube River (Donau
in German) and continue south along the Romantic Road to
Fussen. Drive by Neuschwanstein castle just to sweeten your
dreams before crossing into Austria to get set up at Reutte.

Reutte (pronounced ROY-teh, rolled r), population 5,000, is a
relaxed town, popular with Germans and Austrian for its climate
(doctors recommended its 'grade 1' air), yet it's far from the
international tourist crowd.

If the weather's good, we'll walk to the mysterious castle ruins
and ride the luge. Finish your day off with a slap-dancing bash at
a Tyrolean folk evening.

Sightseeing highlights
● **Dinkelsbuhl**—Just a small Rothenburg without the mobs, but
pretty enough to merit a short stop. Park near the church in the
centre, buy a picnic and just browse. You'll find an interesting
local museum, a well-preserved medieval wall, towers, gates and a
moat.

●● **Ehrenburg ruins**—The ruined castle of Ehrenburg broods over Reutte, capping a nearby hilltop. From the car park, it's a steep 20-minute walk for a great view from your own private ruined castle. For more castle mystique climb 30 minutes more up the larger neighbouring hill to a bigger, more desolate, overgrown, and romantic ruin and imagine how proud Count Meinrad II of Tyrol (who built the castle in 1290) would be to know that his castle repelled 16,000 Swedish soldiers in 1632.

●● **Sommerrodelbahn**—One of the great Alpine experiences is to ride a chair lift up the mountain and 'luge' down riding an oversized skateboard with brakes on a concrete bobsled course. On the Fernpass Road past the ruined castles on the way to Innsbruck are two luge courses. The first is ten minutes past the ruins—you'll see a chairlift on the right. Twenty minutes further toward Innsbruck, in Biberwier just past Lermoos (the first exit after a long tunnel, or, if you take the small road through Lermoos, turn left at the yellow ski lift sign 50 yards before the Shell station), is a better luge, the longest in Austria—4,000 feet. Both are open 8:30 – 17:00, closed when wet. The concrete course banks on the corners and even a novice can go very, very fast. No one emerges from this experience without a wind-blown hairdo and a smile-creased face.

Just before the longer luge is a great photo stop. Behind the sport and Trachtenstuberl shop is a wooden church dome with a striking Zugspitz backdrop. If you have sunshine and a camera, don't miss it.

●● **Tyrolean Folk Evening**—The Tyroleans share their colourful folk dances, costumes and traditions with visitors by putting on 'folk evenings'. Reutte has two or three a week and if you have the chance be sure to take one in. Your hotel will have

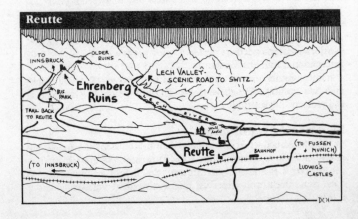

Germany's Romantic Road

the Reutte schedule of events and can call in a reservation for you. They usually start at 20:30 and cost 8 DM (£2.50).

Transport

This is an easy day by car—no big cities, a scenic drive, and the border crossing is usually just a flash of the passport. By train or bus it's trickier. The Romantic Road bus gets into Fussen at 19:35, long after the last bus to Reutte. Those travelling by train will have an easier time riding the bus into Munich and doing Bavaria and Tyrol from there.

Food and accommodation

In July and August Munich and Bavaria are packed with tourists. Tyrol in Austria is easier and a bit cheaper. Reutte is just one of many good home base towns in the area. I choose it because it's not so crowded in peak season, the easy-going locals are always in a party mood, and I like to stay overnight in Austria.

The tourist office should be your first stop in Reutte (one block
in front of the station or 'bahnhof', open Mon – Fri 8:00 – 12:00,
13:00 – 18:00, Sat 8:00 – 12:00, 16:00 – 18:00, Sun 16:00 – 18:00,
tel 05672/2336 or direct from Germany 0043 – 5672/2336. They
are very helpful and can always find you a cheap room (£4.80
($8)) in someone's home. Go over your plans with the T.I., see if
they can book you a folk evening. Pick up a city map.

Reutte has a good little youth hostel (tel 05672 – 3039), and
plenty of reasonable hotels and zimmers. For the youth hostel,
follow the Jugendherberg signs from the town centre, a 10-minute
walk, non-members accepted, clean, rarely full, friendly, open
only 15 June – 25 Aug. I stay at the big central **Hotel Goldener
Hirsch** (from Germany dial 0043 – 5672 – 2508, in Reutte just the
last four digits, ask for Helmut or Monika) which charges £11
($18) per person and serves great £3 ($5) dinners.

In Munich there's a helpful room-finding service in the train
station's tourist information office (open Mon – Sat 8:00 – 23:00,
Sun 13:00 – 21:30, tel 239 – 1259). They can usually find you a
reasonable room near the station. In Oberammergau I enjoyed
friendly budget accommodation and hearty cooking at the
Gasthaus zum Stern (Dorfstrasse 33, 8103 Oberammergau, tel
08822 – 867). They are closed Tuesdays and November, will hold
a room with a phone call, speak English, 54 DM (£17) for a
double. Oberammergau's youth hostel is unfriendly but very good
in all other ways (tel 08822 – 4114). Countryside guesthouses
abound in Bavaria and are a great value. Look for signs that say
'zimmer frei'. The going rate is 42 DM (£13.33) per double
including breakfast.

If Reutte isn't to your liking, nearby Lermoos and idyllic
Nesselwangle are well zimmered. Fussen has lots of rooms—and
many more tourists. The Bavarian countryside around
Neuschwanstein is sprinkled with big farmhouse zimmers. You'll
see plenty of green vacancy signs here.

While the cheapest food in Reutte is at the **SPAR** restaurant
on Mullerstrasse near the station, the classy meals at **Hotel
Goldener Hirsch** are not much more expensive. I like their huge
'Gemuseplate' (vegetables) for 8 DM (£2.50).

TOUR 4

BAVARIA AND CASTLE DAY

Today we circle through the nutcracker and castle corner of Bavaria. After touring Europe's most famous castle, Mad Ludwig's Disney-esque Neuschwanstein, we'll visit Germany's most ornate church, a Rococo riot. Next stop is Oberammergau, Bavaria's wood carving capital and home of the famous passion play, followed by another of Ludwig's extravagant castles—this time the more liveable Linderhof Palace.

Suggested schedule

7:30	Breakfast.
8:15	Leave Reutte.
8:45	Tour Neuschwanstein Castle.
11:30	Picnic by the lake (Alpsee).
12:15	Drive to Wies church and on to Oberammergau.
1:45	Park at Passion Play Theatre, take tour.
3:30	Tour Linderhof Castle (or shopping in Oberammergau).
5:00	Drive home to Reutte via Plansee.
8:30	Tyrolean Folk Evening (if not last night).
Sleep	Reutte.

Transport

This day is designed for drivers. Without your own car it won't be possible. Transport in the area is good but gaps make the proposed circle impossible. Buses go from Reutte to Fussen at 47 past each hour from 8:47 to 17:47. The 8:47 bus goes straight to Ludwig's castle, but others stop at the Fussen station where bus Bf–971 leaves hourly for the castle (2 DM (64p)). The 55-minute train ride connects Munich and Fussen hourly. Buses connect Fussen and Wieskirche only twice a day (6 DM (£1.90)). The Reute–Linderhof–Oberammergau bus leaves at 10:10, stopping from 10:55 to 13:30 at Linderhof, arriving in Oberammergau at 13:55. At 15:10 a bus returns to Reutte getting in at 17:10. Trains connect Reutte and Garmish (7 a day, 1 hour) and Innsbruck (6 a day, 2¾ hours). Hitchhiking is possible, but instead I'd take an all-day bus tour from Munich to cover these sights most efficiently.

Highlights of the Bavarian Circle

It's best to see Neuschwanstein, Germany's most popular castle, early in the morning before the hordes arrive. The castle is open every morning at 9:00. By 10:00 it's packed. Walking up the steep road to the castle you may pass a crazy old bearded Bavarian. (Hug him if you like, he's a photographer's feast, but women beware of his infamous sauerkraut tongue.) Take the English tour and learn the story of Bavaria's Mad King Ludwig. The tour is bare-boned and usually rushed. If possible, read up on Wagner's operas and Ludwig's life before you visit.

After the tour, if you're energetic, climb up to Mary's Bridge for a great view of Europe's 'Disney' castle. The big yellow, more 'lived-in' Hohenschwangau castle nearby was Ludwig's boyhood home. Like its more exciting neighbour, it costs about 6 DM (£1.90) and takes about an hour to tour.

Back down in the village you'll find several restaurants. The self-service Braustuberl is the cheapest, with food that tastes that

Bavaria & Tyrol — The Castle Loop

WEST GERMANY

AUSTRIA

ROMANTIC ROAD TO ROTHENBURG

ECHELSBACHER BRIDGE (GORGE)

STEINGADEN

WIES

AUTOBAHN TO MUNICH

FORGENSEE

OBER-AMMERGAU

TEGELBERG

FÜSSEN

NEUSCHWANSTEIN

HOHENSCHWANGAU

ETTAL

ALPSEE

LINDERHOF

REUTTE

GARMISCH-PARTEN-KIRCHEN

PLANSEE

EHRENBERG RUINS

LUGE

ZUGSPITZE 2973 m

LOUSY ROAD!

GREAT VIEW!

LERMOOS

LUGE

FERNPASS

TUNNEL TO INNSBRÜCK

FALLERSCHEIN

0 KM   5   10
0 MI   5

—D.C.H—

way. Next door is a handy little grocery store. Picnic in the lakeside park. At the crossroad you'll find the best gift shop, the bus stop and international dial-direct-to-home phone booths.

Germany's greatest Rococo-style church, Wies Church, is bursting with beauty just thirty minutes down the road. Go north, turn right at Steingaden, and follow the signs. This church is a droplet of heaven, the final flowering of the Baroque movement. Read about it as you sit in its splendour, then walk back to the car park the long way—through the meadow.

Driving into Oberammergau, take the second left after crossing the river and park near the large modern Passion Play Theatre.

From Oberammergau drive through Garmisch, past Germany's highest mountain, the Zugspitz, into Austria via Lermoos (and the longest luge ride).

Or you can take the small scenic road past Ludwig's Linderhof Castle. It's the most liveable palace I've seen. Incredible grandeur on a homely scale and worth a look if you have the energy and two hours for the tour. Wind past the windsurfer-strewn Plansee, and back into Austria.

Sightseeing highlights

● ● ● **Neuschwanstein**—This is the greatest of King Ludwig II of Bavaria's fairy tale castles. His extravagance and romanticism earned him the title 'Mad King Ludwig'. The obvious inspiration of Disney's castle, it epitomises the Romantic movement of the 19th century. Set on a hilltop with a great view, it's decorated inside and out with lavish damsels in distress, dragons, knights in gleaming armour—respect for the good old Middle Ages. Don't miss it—but miss the crowds by getting there early. Open April–September 9:00–17:30, off season 10:00–16:00. The 6 DM (£1.90) admission includes a mandatory (in English) tour. Often called 'Konigsschlosser' (Royal Castles) on maps, it's in the town of Hohenschwangau, a five minute ride, not counting traffic jams, from Fussen.

● ● **Hohenschwangau**—Much less spectacular and less visited but more lived-in and giving a better look at Ludwig, is his boyhood home castle, yellow and sitting just across the ravine from Neuschwanstein (same hours).

● ● ● **Wies Church**—This lavish pilgrimage church set in a peaceful meadow is a must. Built by Zimmerman in 1750, pilgrims and tourists from around the world enjoy having their breath taken away here. Without a car, it's not worth the headaches. See Wurzburg Chapel or Munich's Asam Church instead.

● ● **Oberammergau**—This very touristy Shirley Temple of Bavarian villages has found a need and filled it. If you like buildings painted with scenery, fine wood carving, plenty of

German cliches on sale and a chance to tour the great 5,000 seat
Passion Play Spielhaus (theatre), this is worth an hour or two.

Actually, the theatre tour (2 DM (64p), one hour tours
throughout the day) is one-of-a-kind fascinating (next Passion Play
is in 1990—watch out!). The carving shops are like wooden art
galleries filled with very expensive whittled works. Visit the
church, a cousin of the Wies, notice the Nazi tombstones in the
graveyard—and get out.

●● **Linderhof**—This is Mad Ludwig's 'home', his most
intimate castle, small and comfortably exquisite—enough for a
minor god. Set in the woods, 15 minutes from Oberammergau,

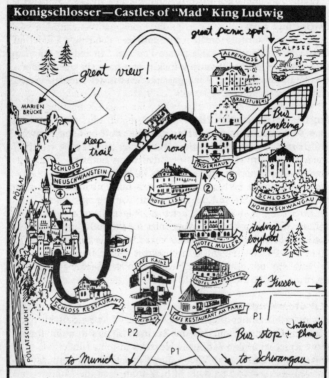

Konigschlosser—Castles of "Mad" King Ludwig

① "OLD BAVARIAN"- HUG HIM, BUT BEWARE OF HIS NOTORIOUS
   SAUERKRAUT TONGUE ☺
② BUS + HORSE CART STOP- FOR RIDE UP TO CASTLE - ITS A
   20 MIN WALK.
③ SMALL GROCERY STORE
④ SCENIC TRAIL DOWN POLLAT GORGE - GORGEOUS!

surrounded by fountains and sculpted, Italian style gardens, it's the only palace I've toured that actually had me feeling envious. Don't miss the grotto. Open April–Sept, 9:00–17:00, off season 9:00–16:00, July and Aug til 17:30. English tours constantly. Plan to stop for two hours. There's a fair amount of walking.

● **Tegelberg Gondola**—Just north of Neuschwanstein, for 16 DM (£5.30) this lift will carry you high above the castle to that peak's 5,500-foot summit. On a clear day you get great views of the Alps and Bavaria and the thrill of watching hang gliders. From there it's a lovely 2-hour hike to Ludwig's castle. Tegelberg has a mountain hut with Tolkien atmosphere and 10 DM (£3.20) beds if you'd like to spend the night and do Ludwig's place the next morning. (Last ride is at 17:00.)

Swimming pool—Reutte has an Olympic-quality swimming pool open from 10:00 to 21:00 which might be a good way to cool off after your castle hikes.

●● **Fallerscheim**—A special treat, this extremely remote log cabin village smothered in Alpine goodness is a flower-speckled world of serene slopes, cowbells, river and breeze music. Thunderstorms roll down this valley like a giant's bowling alley, but the pint-sized church on the high ground, blissfully simple after so much Baroque, seems to promise this huddle of houses will remain standing. The people sitting on benches are mostly Austrian holidaymakers who've rented cabins here. For a rugged chunk of local Alpine peace, spend a night in the local Matratzenlager (simple loft dorm) 'Almwirtscheft Fallerscheim' run by friendly (but no English spoken) Kerle Erwin, open June–Sept, 6 DM (£1.90) per night, 27 beds, one outhouse, good 8 DM (£2.50) meals, 6671 Weissenbach 119a, b/Reutte, tel 05678–5142. Crowded only on weekends. Fallerscheim (at 4,000 feet altitude) is at the end of a miserable 2-mile fit-for-jeep-or-hire-car-only gravel road near Namlose on the Berwang road south of Reutte.

Itinerary options

Train travellers may prefer doing 'castle day' as a side trip from Munich. Organised tours do the Bavarian biggies in a day (the Grey Line, tel 5904–248, does Neuschwanstein, Linderhof, Oberammergau, and the Wies Church in a busy ten hour day for 46 DM (£15), departing daily at 8:30 from near the Munich station). Staying in Reutte may not be worth the transport headaches for those without cars.

Remember, the luge experience is possible only on dry days. It fits easily into Tours 3, 4 or 5.

If you're skipping Vienna, do Munich first, then Reutte, then follow the lovely Lech River valley into Switzerland.

TOUR 5

REUTTE TO MUNICH

Today we'll drive past Germany's highest peak, possibly stopping for a little more Bavarian sightseeing and lunch at a monastery that serves the best beer in Deutschland and then arriving in Munich in time to set up, get our bearings, see the centre of Bavaria's leading city and enjoy some beerhall fun in the evening.

Munich, Germany's most lively city, is also one of its most historic, artistic and entertaining. It's big and growing—with a population of over 1,500,000. Just a little more than a century ago, it was the capital of an independent Bavaria. Its imperial palaces, jewels and grand boulevards constantly remind visitors that this was once a political as well as cultural powerhouse.

Suggested schedule	
8:00	Leave Reutte.
9:00	Ride to the summit of the Zugspitz if weather and budget permit.
11:00	Drive to Andechs for lunch.
14:00	Arrive in Munich, stop at T.I., and check into hotel.
15:30	Explore the heart of town, subway to Odeonsplatz, tour Cuvillies Theatre, see 17:00 glockenspiel at Marienplatz, shopping, browsing, stroll through centre, drop into Hofbrauhaus.
20:00	Dinner and evening of oom-pah fun at Mauthaser's beer hall.
Sleep	Munich.

Sightseeing highlights

● ● **Zugspitz**—Germany's tallest mountain, 10,000 feet, is on the Austrian border. Lifts from both sides take you to the summit where you can mingle back and forth over the border enjoying an incredible view. There are restaurants, shops, telescopes, etc. on top. The lift from the German side departs hourly, takes 75 minutes, costs 44 DM (£14). From the 'Talstation Obermoos', above the Austrian village of Erwald, it's faster, 20% cheaper, and less crowded, but is tricky without your own car. The old gondola (built in 1926—notice the historic displays) leaves every

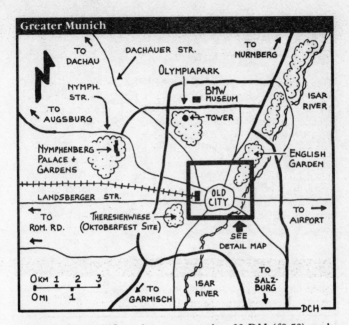

Greater Munich

seven minutes and if you have a sunny day, 30 DM (£9.50), and
90 extra minutes, the Tiroler Zugspitzbahn is worthwhile.
●● **Andechs**—How does a fine Baroque church in a Bavarian
setting at a monastery that serves hearty food and the best beer in
Germany in a carnival setting full of partying locals sound?
That's the soon-to-be-discovered Andechs monastery hiding
happily between two lakes just south of Munich. Come with an
appetite—the food is great—chunks of tender pork chain-sawed
especially for you, huge and soft pretzels (best I've had), spiralled
white radishes, savoury sauerkraut, and Andecher beer that lives
up to its reputation. Everything is served in medieval
proportions—two people can split a meal. Great picnic centre,
too. Open daily 9:00 – 21:00, second class prices, first class view.
Munich sights—See listing for the next tour.
Overrated sights—The Ettal monastery is just another pretty
Baroque face with a knack for commercialism. Garmisch-
Partenkirchen is worth stopping at only if you're in the US Army
and have no choice.

Munich orientation
If you stop at Andechs, a small road takes you into town.
Otherwise you'll be taking the autobahn from Garmisch. Follow
signs to 'Zentrum' and 'Hauptbahnhof'. Munich is a terrible city

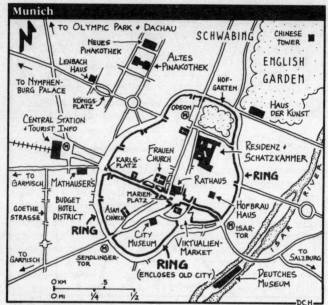

to drive in, so ideally, you'll go straight to the station, find your room within a few streets of there, and leave your car until it's time to go to Salzburg when you'll head out the way you came in, following the Salzburg autobahn signs.

Munich is big—Germany's third largest city—and growing fast, but its excellent tourist information and sleek subway system make life easy for the 5 million visitors who come to town each year.

Take full advantage of the T.I. in the train station (open 8:00–23:00 daily, tel 239–1259, opposite platform 11). Have a list of questions ready, confirm your sightseeing plans, and pick up brochures (30 pf (10p) city map, how to use the public transport, lists of sights, calendar of events, and the young people's guide—get one regardless of your age). If necessary, take advantage of their room finding service. For recorded museum info call 239174, and for sights info: 239175. Train info: 592991.

The great Munich tram, bus and subway system is a sight in itelf. Subways are called U- or S-bahns. The fares are complicated and three rides will cost you the same as a 24-hour pass so spend 6.50 DM (£2.10), sign it, validate it in a machine and you have Munich by the tail for a day (on sale at tourist offices, subway booths and in machines at most stops). The entire system works on the same tickets. Taxis are very expensive and needless.

Orientate yourself in Munich with the Hauptbahnhof – Karlstor – Kaufingerstrasse – Marienplatz – Isartor axis. Most sights are within a few streets of this lovely walk.

You'll find Munich a bit sterile since most of it, including many of the historic buildings, has been rebuilt since the WWII bombings. Its hotels are expensive, but after that, food, fun and transport are cheap.

City telephone code is 089. From Austria dial 050/49/89/and the local number. Most Munich sights are closed on Mondays.

Food and accommodation

Rooms in Munich are expensive—you can't avoid it. Youth hostels strictly enforce their 26-year-old age limit and seeing the city as a side-trip is poor value for money. But there are plenty of good rooms, most located within a few streets of the Hauptbahnhof (central train station) with its excellent room finding service. Ideally, call ahead and reserve one of the places I've listed below. Otherwise, use the T.I.

The info people hate the word 'cheap'. They recommend rooms selectively and can normally get mid-day arrivals an 80 DM (£25) double in a pension. The best budget rooms are near the station. Evening arrivals may be stuck in a 110 DM (£35) hotel room. Even dormitory type flophouses cost well over 20 DM (£6.50) per person.

Hotel Gebhardt on Goethestrasse 38, 8000 Munich 2, just three minutes from the station was the best combination of neighbourhood, comfort and price I could find. 65 DM (£21) doubles, English spoken, tel 089/539446 or 539585. With shower, 95 DM (£30), some cheaper 3- and 4-bed rooms.

Pension Monopteros on Oettingenstrasse 35, overlooking the Englischer Garten is not so central but more peaceful. On a tram line, simple, friendly, tel 292348, 100 DM (£32) doubles.

International Haus on Elisabethstrasse 87, tel 089/185081 offers 600 beds in depressing 5-bed rooms. 27 DM (£8.50) per person, they'll hold a room with a phone call, normally has beds available. Easy to find, easy parking.

Jugendhotel Marienherberg is a very pleasant, friendly convent accepting young women only (18 – 25 year age limit) charging 25 DM (£8) per person in 5 – bed rooms. Very close to station at Goethestrasse 9, tel 089/555891.

YMCA (CVJM) is open to people of all ages and sexes. Very central, just two blocks south of the station at Landwehrstrasse 13, tel 089/555951, charging about 32 DM (£10) per person in a double, this is a great bet if you can get a spot.

Munich's Youth Hostels charge about 16 DM (£5) and strictly limit admission to YH members who are under 27. If you qualify, call 723650 or 7236550.

'The Tent', Munich's International Youth Camp 'Kapuzinerholzl' offers a place on the wooden floor of a huge circus tent with a mattress, blankets, good showers and free tea in the morning for 5DM (£1.50) to anyone under 23. Call 1414300 before heading out. No curfew. Take the U-bahn 1 to Rotkreuzplatz, catch tram No. 12 to Botanischer Garten, and follow the youthful crowd down Franz-Schrankstrasse to the big tent. This is near the Nymphenburg palace. Open from the end of June through August.

The best budget food in Munich is in the beerhalls. There are many to choose from but I prefer the **Mauthaser Bierstadt** at 5 Bayerstrasse halfway between the Hauptbahnhof (train station) and Karlstor. The atmosphere is thick, the fat and shiny-leather band even has church mice standing up and conducting ¾ time with a breadstick. Meals cost 10 DM (£3.20) (I like the schweinwurst and kraut), huge litre beers (called 'ein Mass') are 6 DM (£1.90), white radishes are salted and cut in delicate spirals and huge beermaids pull mustard packets from their cavernous cleavages.

The most famous beerhall, the **Hofbrauhaus**, is much more touristy. But do drop in—it's fun to see 200 Japanese drinking beer in a German beerhall. Many beerhalls are closed Mondays.

For outdoor atmosphere and a cheap meal, spend an evening at the **Englischer Garten's Chinese Pagoda** bierstadt. You're welcome to bring your own food and grab a table or buy from picnic stall ('brotziet') right there. 6,000 seats!

For university atmosphere, cheap food, beer and crowded basements of conversation, head out to the **Studentenstadt** (University dorm) bierstuben.

The fastest cheap and central meal is found at **Mauthaser's** stand-up self-serve bar (facing Bayerstrasse) or at the lively open-air **Viktualien Market,** just behind Marienplatz. Plenty of good picnic material here.

The classiest picnic of the tour can be purchased in the historic elegant—and expensive—**Alois Dallmayr** delicatessen at 15 Dienerstrasse just behind the Rathaus. Wander through this dieter's purgatory, put together a royal picnic and eat it in the nearby, and adequately royal, Hofgarten. To save money, browse at Dallmayr's but buy in the basement of the Kaufhof across Marienplatz.

TOUR 6

MUNICH

We'll spend all day immersed in the art and history of this cultural hub of Germany. To see this exciting Bavarian capital in less than two days requires selectivity and careful planning. Today will include a mountain of Baroque razzle-dazzle, crown jewels, great art and biergarten fun.

Suggested schedule

8:00	Breakfast.
9:00	Munchner Stadtmuseum, Viktualien market (buy picnic here or at Alois Dallmayr).
11:00	Tour Residenz and Schatzkammer.
12:30	Picnic in Hofgarten, walk to Alte Pinakothek.
13:30	Alte Pinakothek.
15:30	Haus der Kunst or free time.
17:00	Stroll through Englischer Garten, early dinner or a drink at the Chinese Pagoda.

Sightseeing highlights

● ● **Marienplatz and the Pedestrian Zone**—The essence of Munich is best experienced as the escalator takes you out of the underground system and into the sunlit Marienplatz. Surrounding you is the glory of Munich—great buildings bombed flat and rebuilt—the ornate facades of the new and old City Halls (Altes Rathaus), outdoor cafes, and people bustling and lingering like the birds and breeze they share this square with. From here the pedestrian mall (Kaufingerstrasse and Neuhauserstrasse) leads you through a great shopping area past plenty of fun street singers, the towering Frauenkirche (with its 350-foot high viewpoint), and several fountains, to Karlstor and the train station. The old glockenspiel 'jousts' as it has for generations on Marienplatz daily at 11:00, 12:00 and 17:00. (If you like the Rothenburg Meistertrunk show, you'll love this one!)
● ● **Residenz**—For a good dose of imperial Bavarian grandeur, tour the palace of the Wittelsbach family. Different wings are open in the morning and afternoon but either tour is ample. For 600 years the Wittelsbachs ruled Bavaria from here. Don't miss the Schatzkammer (treasury), a thousand years of Wittelsbach heirlooms, which, like the palace, is open Tues—Sat

10:00 – 16:30, Sun 10:00 – 13:00. Take U-3, or 6 to Odeonsplatz or walk from Mary's Place.

●● **The Cuvillies Theatre**—Attached to the Residenz, this National Theatre designed by Cuvillies, is dazzling enough to send you back to the days of the divine monarch. Open Mon – Sat 14:00 – 17:00, Sun 10:00 – 17:00.

● **Munchner Stadtmuseum**—The underrated Munich city museum just a few blocks off Marienplatz is a pleasant surprise— great old photography exhibition, historic puppets, the story of beer, the world's largest collection of musical instruments and the best collection of Jugendstil art (Art Nouveau) I've seen. Bored and very playful guards, no crowds. Open 9:00 – 16:30, closed Mondays.

●● **Alte Pinakothek**—Bavaria's best collection of art, stored in a pleasing easy-to-handle museum. Strong on Italian and North European artists, Durer and Rubens. Open 9:00 – 16:30, closed Monday, open 19:00 – 21:00 on Tues and Thurs. Take U-8 to Konigsplatz.

● **Haus der Kunst**—Built by Hitler as a temple of Nazi art, this bold and fascist building now houses modern art—much of which the Fuhrer censored. It's a fun collection—Kandinsky, Picasso, Dali, and much more from this century. Open 9:00 – 16:30, closed Mondays. Take U-3, 5 or 6 to Odeonsplatz and a peaceful walk through the Hofgarten and past the 'Kriegerdenkmal'—a bombed building left as a war memorial. (Or, take bus 53, 55, or Tram 20.)

Bayerisches Nationalmuseum—An interesting collection of Riemenschneider carvings, manger scenes, traditional living rooms and old Bavarian house. Open 9:00 – 17:00, closed Mondays. Take tram 20, bus 53 or 55.

● **Deutsches Museum**—This German answer to our Science Museum has everything of scientific and technical interest from astronomy to zymurgy. This museum can be disappointing due to its overwhelming size and lack of English descriptions. Pick up the 4 DM (£1.25) 'guide through the collections', skip the German-only planetarium, and focus on the lower floors where you'll find more English info. With ten miles of exhibits you'll need to be selective. Lots of hands-on gadgetry but the collections seem to have been left in the dust by the computer age. Self-serve cafeteria. Open 9:00 – 17:00, 5 DM (£1.60) admission. S-Bahn to Isartorplatz or tram 18. Despite its reputation, unless you are (or wish you were) an engineer, two hours is enough time here.

Schwabing—Munich's artsy and Bohemian university district has been called 'not a place but a state of mind'. That may have been a compliment but all I experienced was a mental lapse. The Bohemians run the boutiques and I think the most colourful thing

about Schwabing is the road leading back downtown. U-3 or 6
will take you to the Munchener – Freiheit Centre if you want to
wander. Most jazz and disco joints are near Occamstrasse.

● **Englischer Garten**—One of Europe's great parks, this 'Hyde
Park' of Munich is the Continent's largest, laid out in 1789 by an
American. Bikes are for hire at the south entrance, and there's a
huge beer garden near the Chinese Pagoda. Caution: nude
sunbathers. A very rewarding respite from the city.

Asam Church—Near the Stadtmuseum, this private church of
the Asam brothers shows off their very popular Baroque-
concentrate style. If you missed (or loved) the Wies Church, visit
the masterpiece by these two Rococonuts.

● **Olympic Grounds**—Munich's great 1972 Olympic stadium
and sports complex is now a fine park offering a tower
(commanding but rather boring view, 8:00 – 24:00, 4 DM (£1.25)),
excellent swimming pool (open to the public 7:00 – 22:00,
Mondays 10:00 – 22:00, 4 DM (£1.25)), a good look at its striking
'cobweb' style of architecture, and plenty of sun, grass and picnic
potential. Easy access on the U-3 or 8 to Olympiazentrum.

BMW Museum—Fascinating only to yuppies or those who are
into cars, the BMW headquarters, located in a striking building
across the street from the Olympic Grounds, offers free factory
tours and a museum. Sign up for an English tour and spend your
wait touring the museum.

●● **Nymphenburg Palace**—This royal summer palace is
mediocre if you've already seen the Residenz. If you do tour it
don't miss King Ludwig's 'Gallery of Beauties'—a room stacked
with portraits of Bavaria's loveliest women—according to Ludwig.
(Notice his taste for big noses.) The palace park, good for a royal
stroll, contains the tiny Amalienburg palace, a Rococo jewel of a
hunting lodge by Cuvillies. The sleigh and coach collection
(Marstallmuseum) is especially interesting for Mad Ludwig fans.
The palace cafeteria is reasonably priced. Open 9:00 – 12:30,
13:30 – 17:00, closed Mondays, shorter hours Oct – March.
Admission 5 DM (80p) use the 2.50 DM (£1.60), English
guidebook. Take the U-1 and then tram 12 toward
Amalienburgstrasse, to Schloss Nymphenburg.

●● **Dachau**—Since we plan to visit the even more powerful
Mauthausen concentration camp, I haven't worked Dachau into
our schedule. But if you won't be touring Mauthausen on your
way to Vienna, please visit Dachau. Dachau was the first Nazi
concentration camp (1933). Today it is the most accessible camp
to travellers and is a very effective voice from the recent but
grisly past, warning and pleading 'Never Again'—the memorial's
theme. This is a valuable experience, and when approached
thoughtfully is well worth the drive—in fact, it may change your

life. See it. Feel it. Read and think about it. After this most
powerful sightseeing experience, many people gain a respect for
history and are inspired to learn more about contemporary
injustices, and work against tragic recurrences.

Upon arrival, pick up the mini-guide and notice when the next
documentary film in English will be shown (normally at 11:30
and 15:30). The museum and the film are worthwhile. Notice the
Expressionist fascist-inspired art near the theatre. Outside, be sure
to tour the reconstructed barracks and the memorial shrines at the
far end. (Near the theatre are English books, slides and a good
w.c. The camp is open 9:00–17:00, closed on Mondays.)

Take the S-bahn 2 to Dachau and catch bus 722 (Dachau-Ost)
from the station to Gedenkstatte. If you're driving,
Dachauerstrasse leads from central Munich to Dachau, follow the
K2—Gedenkstatte signs. Open Tues–Sun 9:00–17:00. (Note:
train travellers should see Dachau rather than Mauthausen.)

Oktoberfest—While you can always find a festival in Munich's
beerhalls, the entire city celebrates each autumn with this greatest
of beer parties. Starting the third Saturday of every September
and roasting the last ox two weeks later, this mammoth festival is
an experience of a lifetime. It's crowded, but arrive in the
morning and the T.I. will find you a room. The fairgrounds known as
the 'Wies'n' (a few blocks from the station) erupt in a frenzy of
rides, dancing, strangers strolling arm in arm down rows of picnic
tables, and tons of beer, pretzels and wurst in a bubbling
cauldron of fun. The 'three loops' roller-coaster must be the
greatest on earth (do it *before* the beerdrinking). During the fair,
the city functions even better than normal and it's a good time to
sightsee even if beerhall rowdiness isn't your cup of tea. The
Fasching carnival time before Lent is nearly as wild.

TOUR 7

MUNICH TO SALZBURG

After a free morning to do any last sightseeing or exploring in
Munich, we'll take the autobahn two hours south back into
Austria, setting up in Salzburg by mid-afternoon. Today's
sightseeing plan is flexible. There are four major sights and you
must pick two—the Nymphenburg Palace and the Deutsches
Museum in Munich and the Berchtesgaden Salt Mines and the
Hellbrunn castle near Salzburg. Speed maniacs with a car could
do three but I'd rather do two and get comfortably set up to take
a rest before a hopefully music-filled Salzburg evening.

Suggested schedule

9:00	Check out of hotel. Tour Nymphenburg Palace or the Deutsches Museum.
11:30	Drive south, picnicking en route.
14:00	Tour the Berchtesgaden salt mines or the Hellbrunn castle.
17:00	Arrive in Salzburg, visit T.I., check into hotel.
19:30	Stroll through gardens to Augustiner Keller for dinner, floodlit city-from-the-bridge view for dessert.
22:00	Wander the streets of old Salzburg.

AUSTRIA

32,000 square miles.
7.6 million people (235 per square mile and holding).
One schilling = 5p; £1 = 22.1 AS.

Austria during the grand old Hapsburg days was Europe's most
powerful empire. Its royalty put together that giant empire of
more than 50 million people by making love, not war—having lots
of children and marrying them into the other royal houses of
Europe.

Today Austria is a small landlocked country that does more to
cling to its elegant past than any other in Europe. The waltz is
still the rage and Austrians are very sociable. More so than
anywhere else, it's important to greet people you pass on the
streets or meet in shops. The Austrian's version of 'hello' is a
cheerful 'Gruss Gott!' (May God be with you). You'll get the
correct pronunciation after the first volley—listen and copy.

While they speak German and German money is readily accepted in Salzburg, Innsbruck and Reutte, the Austrians cherish their distinct cultural and historical traditions. They are not Germans. Austria is mellow and relaxed compared to Deutschland. 'Gemutlichkeit' is the special local word for this special Austrian cosy-and-easy approach to life. It's good living—either engulfed in mountain beauty or swirling in high culture. The people like to stroll as if every day were Sunday, topping things off with a visit to a coffee or pastry shop.

While the Austrians make less money per year than their neighbours, they work less (34 hours a week) and live longer (14 per cent of the people are senior citizens, the highest percentage in the world). Austria is technically part of Eastern Europe and therefore not in NATO or the EEC.

Austrians eat at about the same times as we do. Treats include Wiener Schnitzel (breaded veal cutlet), Knodel (dumplings), Apfelstrudel and fancy desserts. White wines, Heuriger (new wine) and coffee are delicious and popular. Shops are open from 8 am – 5 pm. Banks keep roughly the same hours, but usually close for lunch.

Transport

By car leave Munich the way you came in, heading away from town on Bayerstrasse and following the autobahn signs to Salzburg—just 60 miles to the southeast. You'll pass Herrenchiemsee on your left and the very first autobahn rest area built during Hitler's rule and frescoed with 'Deutschland uber alles' themes (take the Feldon exit, presently a lakeside US military hotel). After crossing the border stay on the autobahn curving south in the direction of Hallein before taking the

Salzburg exit at Anif. This road leads you north into town passing first the Schloss Hellbrunn and then the Tourist Info. Ask the T.I. for advice on locating your hotel and parking. Don't even try to drive in the old town. Park your car and walk or use the bus system.

By train it's an easy 90-minute trip to Salzburg. Use the Salzburg station T.I. and catch a city bus from there to Hellbrunn if you like (Bus H, departing at 10 and 40 past each hour, 12 AS (60p), 15-minute ride). For Berchtesgaden, take the train direct from Munich, easy and scenic bus connection into Salzburg.

Sightseeing highlights

● **Berchtesgaden**—This Alpine resort flaunts its attractions very effectively and you may find yourself in a traffic jam of desperate tourists looking for ways to turn their money into fun. From the station and the helpful T.I. (tel 08652/5011) buses go to the idyllic Konigsee (2-hour scenic cruises, 15 DM (£4.75)) and the salt mine (a 30-minute walk otherwise).

The salt mines—the best of four regional mines I've toured—are open daily 8:00 – 17:00 (winter, Mon – Fri 12:30 – 15:30). For 12 DM (£3.80) you put on the traditional miners' outfits, get on funny little trains and go zipping deep into the mountain. For 90 minutes you'll cruise subterranean lakes, slide speedily down long wooden (splinter-free) bannisters, and learn how they mined salt so long ago.

Hitler's famous 'eagle's nest' towered high above Berchtesgaden. Now Kehlstein and Obersalzburg are open to visitors but little of Hitler's Alpine retreat remains (he only went there five times) and the ride up the private road costs about 16 DM (£5).

● **Hellbrunn Castle**—The real attraction here is a garden of clever trick fountains and the sadistic joy the tour guide gets by soaking the tourists in his group. The archbishop's palace is hardly worth a look, his garden is pretty enough, but bring a raincoat and dive into the bubbly tour. Open 9:00 – 17:30 daily, 6 DM (£1.90) for the tour, three miles south of Salzburg just off the road as you enter, or bus H from downtown.

Salzburg sights—See next tour.

Salzburg orientation

Salzburg, with a well-preserved old town, gardens, churches, lush surroundings, set under Europe's biggest intact medieval castle and forever smiling to the tunes of Mozart and *The Sound of Music,* is a town that knows how to be popular.

This city of 140,000 is divided into old and new. The old town sitting between two hills straddling the river holds all the charm

and is served by a fine bus system (12 AS (60p) ride, 3 rides =
the cost of a 24 hour pass). The T.I. office (at the train station,
on Mozartplatz in the old centre, and on the highway entrance to
the city) is your essential first stop. When you arrive at the T.I.
get a room, confirm your plans, and have your list of questions
answered. Ask for a map, sights list, youth in Salzburg booklet,
and a schedule of events. Try to book a concert for this evening.
If you missed the folk evening in Reutte, you may catch one
tonight.

Food and accommodation

Finding a room in Salzburg—even during the Music Festival—is
easy. The tourist offices can give you a pamphlet listing all the
pensions, hostels and private rooms in town, or they can find you
a 20 DM (£6.30) bed in the neighbourhood of your choice.

Zimmers, or private rooms, abound. They cost about 20 DM
(£6.30) per person and are cosy but normally far from the centre.
Use the T.I.

Salzburg's **youth hostels** are excellent and have no age limit.
Call 75030 (July and Aug), 842670 (all year), 76241 (April–Sept).
Most charge about 90 AS (£4) and start checking in at 17:00.

Institute St Sebastian—It's usually easy to get a room here.
Friendly, clean, great historic location next to graveyard with
Mozart's mom, £14 doubles, £5.60 per dormitory bed, breakfast
extra, those with sheets save 15 AS (75p). Will hold a room with
a phone call. On Linzer Gasse 41, directly across river from the
old town. Tel. 71386.

Zum Junger Fuchs—Great location, incredible old building,
cheap, plain, elderly management, 300 AS (£13.50) doubles, no
breakfast, showers extra. Across from Institute St Sebastian at
Linzer Gasse 54, tel 75496.

Salzburg boasts many fun and atmospheric places to eat. My
favourite is the **Augustiner Braustuble** at Augustinergasse 4
(walk through the Mirabellgarten, over the Mullnersteg bridge
and ask for help). This place is so rustic and crude that I hesitate
to show my true colours by recommending it but I must. It's like
a Munich beerhall without the music, a historic setting with beer-
sloshed smoke-stained halls, and a pleasant outdoor beer garden
serving another fine local monastic brew. Local students mix with
tourists here eating hearty slabs of schnitzel with their fingers or
cold meals from the picnic counter. 1,000 seats, open daily
15:00–23:00. It'll bring out the barbarian in you. For dessert
enjoy the incomparable floodlit view from the nearby pedestrian
bridge. More central and normal (and not as fun) is the
Stiftskeller St Peter or **Peterkeller** next to St Peter's church
and Mouchsberg.

TOUR 8

SALZBURG AND THE SALZKAMMERGUT

Today we'll enjoy the sights of Salzburg and spend the afternoon in *Sound of Music* country—the Salzkammergut Lake District— spending the night in the postcard pretty fjord-cuddling town of Hallstatt.

Suggested schedule

9:00	Tour Hohensalzburg—the castle.
10:45	Visit Glockenspiel as it performs or tour festival houses.
12:00	Picnic, check out of hotel.
14:00	Drive into Lakes District.
	Afternoon and evening free in Hallstatt (or train travellers will stay in Salzburg and take 14:00 *Sound of Music* Tour for a look at the lakes).
Sleep	Hallstatt.

Transport

Everything in Salzburg today can be done on foot. When you're ready to depart, by car leave Salzburg on the Grazer Bundesstrasse (up Linzer Gasse, over the tracks, right on Minnesheimstrasse, and wind out of town following signs to Gaisberg, Fuschlsee and St Gilgen). A detour up the Gaisberg takes you to a 3,800-foot summit and a good view. This is the *Sound of Music* country (alias the Salzkammergut Lake District).

The road to Hallstatt leads past St Gilgen (pleasant but touristy) to Bad Ischl, the centre of the Salzkammergut (with a spa, salt mine tour, casino and good tourist office (tel 06132-3520)), a tiny 600-year-old roadside watermill just north of the town of Au (worth a look), and along Hallstattersee to Hallstatt. Park in the middle of the tunnel, you'll see a 'P' sign and a waterfall. Walk down into town from there. This car park is free, affords a fine view of the town and lake, and parking in town is frustrating.

While the Salzammergut is well served by trains and buses, I'd recommend that train travellers see it from the window of the *Sound of Music* tour (described later), spend the night in Salzburg again and take the early train toward Vienna. If you do take the

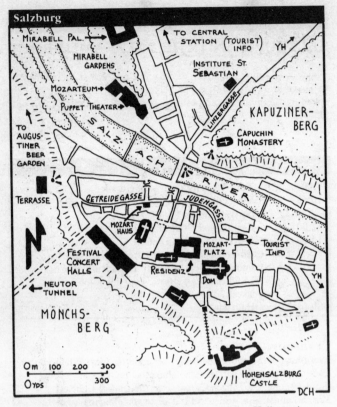

time to train into the Salzkammergut, the ride to Hallstatt is gorgeous and the thrilling finale is a boat ride that connects the town with its station across the lake.

Sightseeing highlights
● ● **Fortress Hohensalzburg**—This castle so dominates Salzburg's skyline that a visit is almost required. The interior is so-so and the tour not worth your time. But the view is great and it's fun to romp around Europe's greatest medieval fortress. The funicular will zip you effortlessly to the top (21 AS (95p) round-trip, rides leave constantly). Open daily, 10 AS (50p) entrance, 30 AS (£1.50) with tour.

● **City Walking Tour**—A great one-hour 50 AS (£2.25) guided walking tour of the old town leaves from the T.I at Mozartplatz daily at 12:15 (May – October).

● ● **Sound of Music Tour**—I took this tour sceptically (as part

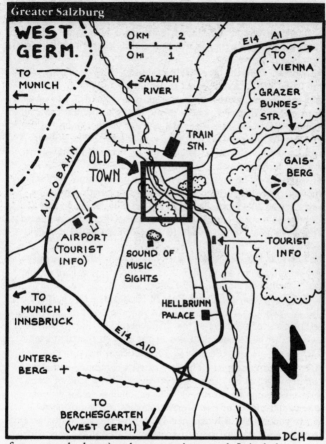

Greater Salzburg

WEST GERM.

TO MUNICH

0 KM 2
0 MI 1

SALZACH RIVER

E14 A1

TO VIENNA

GRAZER BUNDES-STR

AUTOBAHN

TRAIN STN.

OLD TOWN

GAIS-BERG

AIRPORT (TOURIST INFO)

SOUND OF MUSIC SIGHTS

TOURIST INFO

TO MUNICH + INNSBRUCK

HELLBRUNN PALACE

E14 A10

UNTERS-BERG

TO BERCHESGARTEN (WEST GERM.)

DCH

of my research chores) and was very impressed. It includes a quick but good general city tour, hits all the S.O.M. spots (including the gazebo, the stately home and the wedding church), and shows you a lovely stretch of the Salzkammergut. The Salzburg Panorama Tours Company charges 220 AS (£10) for the 3½ hour tour which leaves from Mirabellplatz daily at 9:30 and 14:00. Telephone 74029 for a reservation and a free pick-up from your hotel if you like. This is worthwhile for S.O.M. fans without a car or who won't otherwise be going into the Salzkammergut. Warning: The bus is entirely full of Americans singing 'Doh—a Deer', and 'Climb Every Mountain'.

●●● **Salzburg Festival**—Each summer from late July to early September, Salzburg hosts its famous Salzburger Festspiele. This

is a fun and festive time to be in Salzburg and, while it's
crowded, there are plenty of beds and usually some tickets
available the day of the concert. Salzburg is busy with concerts in
its palaces and churches year round and if you want music, this is
the place to come.

● **Mozart's Birthplace (Geburtshaus)**—Maybe it's just me,
but I find birthplaces of famous people are usually as dead as
they are. This is almost a pilgrimage though, and if you loved
Amadeus you'll have to check it out. Right in the old town on
colourful Getreidegasse, open daily 9:00 – 19:00, 30 AS (£1.35).

● **Getreidegasse**—Old Salzburg's main street, this is a very
lively and colourful street famous for its many old guild signs,
and still looking much like it did in Mozart's day.

● **Carillon**—The bell tower on Mozartplatz chimes throughout
the day. The man behind the bells gives fascinating tours on
weekdays at 10:45 and 17:45. You'll actually be up on top among
35 bells as the big barrels turns, the music flies, and you learn
what a 'dingbat' is. Buy your 10 AS (50p) tickets 10 minutes
early.

● **Festival Houses**—The great concert halls of the Salzburg
festival offer tours at 11:00 and 15:00 Mon – Fri except during
the festival. Worthwhile.

● **Mirabell Gardens and Palace (Schloss)**—The gardens are
always open and free but really to enjoy the lavish palace try to
get a ticket to a concert in the 'Mirabellschloss'—Baroque music
contained in a Baroque hall is a happy bird in the right cage.
Tickets are around 180 AS (£8.50) (students, half price).

●● **Salzkammergut**—This is Austria's commune-with-nature
country. Idyllic, majestic, but not rugged. It's a land of lakes,
forested mountains, storybook villages, endless walking oppor-
tunies, and plenty of cheap private homes and youth hostels.
While you could easily zimmer down here and make this area the
focus of your trip we are just sneaking it in quickly, content to
get in a representative taste and a very pleasant and restful
evening.

●●● **Hallstatt**—Our target is Hallstatt—a town whose photograph always draws desirous gasps when I show it to my travel
classes. Hallstatt is tiny, bullied onto a ledge by a selfish
mountain and a lovely lake. It can be toured on foot in about 10
minutes.

The T.I. (tel 06134-208, daily 9:30 – 16:30) can find you a room
and point you wherever you'd like. The humble museum adjacent
to the T.I. is interesting since little Hallstatt was the centre of
this part of Europe in 1000 BC. Celtic tribes dug for precious
salt here and there have been many interesting finds here from
what archaeologists all over the world call the 'Hallstatt Period'.

The church cemetery in town is so old that the bones of the long dead had to make way for the newly dead. The result is a fascinating chapel of bones. This is the only opportunity bone fans will have on this tour to see the real thing.

The nearby Dachstein Caves are famous but not worth our time or money. The Hallstatt salt mine tour is fun but tedious. You'll ride a frighteningly steep funicular high above the town, take a short walk, do the same old miners' underground train routine as at Berchtesgaden and listen to a German-only tour. The publicised ancient Celtic graveyard excavation sites are a real disappointment.

The charm of Hallstatt is the village and lakeside setting. Go there to relax, eat, walk and paddle. Note: In August tourist crowds trample most of Hallstatt's charm.

Accommodation

The T.I. can almost always find you a room. Only August—especially the first two weeks—is bad. There are plenty of zimmers generally charging 150 AS (£6.75) night. Some will charge quite a bit more for stays less than three nights.

Gasthoff Simony—My favourite, with a lake view, balconies, creaky wood floors, antique furniture, stocking-feet tidy, right on the square, 380 AS (£17) per double. Call Susan Scheutz at 06134/231 for a reservation. Address: 4830 Hallstatt.

Pension Sarstein—At Gosaumuhlstrasse 83, tel 217, good central location with a view, 150 AS (£6.75) person.

The Naturefreunde-Herberge—At Kirchenweg 36 just below the car park, tel 318, but absolutely no English spoken, 100 AS (£4.50) per person in 6-bed rooms. Open all year, a good value. ('Nature's friends houses' are found throughout the Alps. They are cheap, good, fun and basic.)

The Youth Hostel—On Salzburgstrasse just below the salt mine lift, clean, very simple, 40 AS (£1.80), tel 681 or 279. Open 15 May – 15 Sept.

The nearby village of Obertraun is a peaceful alternative to Hallstatt in August. You'll find plenty of zimmers and a luxurious youth hostel.

Itinerary options

Two nights in a row in Salzburg with the S.O.M. bus tour for a look at the lakes district is best for those travelling by train. But if you're feeling good and energetic, try to spend the night in Hallstatt. If you prefer rivers to lakes and have had enough of Salzburg by noon, take to the road for the Danube River valley and spend the evening in a quite different, more eastern-feeling world on a river that could float you all the way to Russia.

TOUR 9

HALLSTATT TO VIENNA

Today we head to our tour's easternmost point, travelling as
quickly as possible to the Danube River where we'll tour the
powerful Mauthausen concentration camp and explore the
romantically ruined castles, vineyards, glorious abbeys and scenery
of the Danube's Wachau Valley. By dinnertime we'll be checked
into our Vienna hotel and ready to experience Paris' eastern rival,
the Hapsburg capital—Vienna.

Suggested schedule	
8:00	Hallstatt (or Salzburg) early departure.
10:00	Tour Mauthausen Concentration Camp.
12:00	Lunch in village of Mauthausen.
13:00	Danube Valley—riverside or autobahn to Melk. Tour town and abbey, drive to Krems and into Vienna.
17:00	Arrive Vienna, visit tourist information office.
18:00	Check into hotel.
19:00	Stroll through centre with A–Z book. Dinner near Am Hof (maybe at Esterhazykeller), late wine at Brezel Gwolb.
Sleep	Vienna

Transport

Today is very demanding. Drivers will want the earliest start out
from Hallstatt. Follow scenic route 145 through Gmunden to the
autobahn and head east. Just after Linz, take the St Valentine
exit. Follow the Mauthausen signs, cross the Donau (Danube),
turn left, pass Mauthausen town and follow signs to KZ-lager.
From Mauthausen the speedy route is to take the autobahn to
Melk, but if you don't mind the curves and the beauty, follow
route 3 along the river.

This region, from Persenbeug to Melk, is Nibelungengau, the
4th and 5th century home of the legendary Nibelung tribe,
dramatised in Wagner's opera. Next stop: Melk's great abbey.
Cross the bridge and follow the signs not into town but to the
'Benediktinerstif', or abbey (no, Maria wasn't here).

The most scenic stretch of Donau is the Wachau Valley lying
between Melk and Krems. From Melk cross the river again and

stay on route 3. After Krems route 3 is nearly an autobahn
speeding you right into Vienna.

Navigating in Vienna, as in any big European city, is a mess.
Study the map and see the series of 'ringstrasse' looping out from
the Donau. As you approach the city you'll cross the North
Bridge and land right on the 'gurtel'—or outer ring. Circle
around on this thoroughfare until you reach the 'spoke street' you
need. Treat the inner ringstrasse the same way.

Train travellers should skip Mauthausen (Dachau outside of
Munich has much easier public access) and take the train straight
to Melk where you can tour the abbey and picnic on the scenic
Melk – Krems Danube River cruise. Boats leave Melk at 9:00,
12:30 and 14:30. Call the DDSG boat company's office,
0732/270011 in Linz, or 266536 in Vienna, or the Melk T.I. at
02752/2307 to confirm these times. It's a two-hour ride to the
attractive but rather boring town of Krems where you can
connect with an hourly 60-minute train ride into Vienna (there's
quite a walk from the Krems boat dock to train station). Or, you
can stay on board and complete the 5½-hour Melk – Vienna
cruise.

If you take the train directly into Viennas (3½ hours from
Salzburg) you can easily do the Wachau train/boat excursion as a
day trip later on. Remember the six-knot flow of the Donau
makes downstream trips about a third faster.

Sightseeing highlights—Danube Valley
● ● ● **Mauthausen Concentration Camp**—More powerful
and less American-oriented than Dachau, this slave labour and
death camp functioned from 1938 to 1945 'for the exploitation
and extermination of Hitler's opponents'. Over half of its 206,000
quarry-working prisoners were killed here. Set in a strangely
beautiful setting next to the Danube and its now still and
overgrown quarry, Mauthausen is open daily from 8:00 – 17:00.
The camp barracks house a museum (some English labels but it
helps to pick up the English booklet) and a graphic film (top of
each hour, German only, but it doesn't really matter). Go
downstairs for the most emotionally-moving rooms and gas
chamber. The ghosts of the horrors can still be felt. Outside the
camp each victim's country has erected a gripping memorial.
Many yellowed photos sport fresh flowers. Walk to the barbed
wire memorial overlooking the quarry. By touring a concentration
camp and putting ourselves through this emotional wringer we
are heeding and respecting the fervent wish of the victims of this
fascism—that we 'never forget'. Too many people forget by
choosing not to know.
● ● ● **Melk Abbey (Benediktinerstift)**—This newly restored

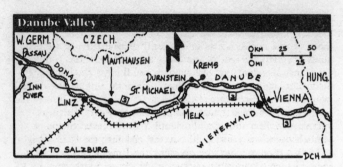

abbey beaming proudly over the Danube Valley is one of
Europe's great sights. Freshly painted and gilded throughout, it's
a Baroque dream, a lily alone. To see its lavish library, church,
palace rooms and the great Danube view from the abbey balcony,
you must take a tour. German ones go constantly, English tours
only with groups of 20 or more. Open daily 9:00 – 12:00 and
13:00 – 17:00, call 02752/2312232 to find out when the next
English group is scheduled (normally at 11:30, other times
haphazardly). The pretty village below makes waiting for a tour
pleasant. (Melk T.I. 02752-2307, fine youth hostel tel 2681).
● ● **Wachau Valley**—A lovely drive or cruise. Good wine
garden and tasting in St Michael for a break. Durnstein is a fly
paper luring hordes of tourists with its traffic free quaintness and
its one claim to fame—and fortune—Richard the Lion Heart was
imprisoned here in 1193. You can probably sleep in his bedroom.

Vienna orientation
Vienna is so big and busy and complex that a little chaos would
be understandable. Even though administrative districts of the city
are called 'Bezirks', the place is very orderly and has gone to
great lengths to make life easy—if not cheap—for its visitors.
    The heart of the city snuggles around the towering St Stephen's
cathedral south of the Donau, held together tightly by the
Ringstrasse. This is the first 'Bezirk'. The 'gurtel' is a broader
ring road containing the rest of the centre, or Bezirks 2 – 9.
Nearly all our sightseeing will be done in the core first district or
along the inner Ringstrasse. As a tourist, concern yourself only
with this small old centre and the city suddenly becomes
manageable.
    Vienna's tourist office, located in front of the Opera House
under the Ringstrasse, is too small and crowded but excellent.
They find rooms and provide visitors with pamphlets on whatever
they need. Stop here first with your sightseeing plan to confirm a
list of needs and questions and pick up a city map, list of

restaurants, museum hours, walking tour schedule, programme of events, Jugendstil flier, transport info and the essential *'Vienna From A to Z'* book. This book is really all you need to see the town. Every important building has a flag banner with a number on it that keys into this little guidebook. Every city should spoil its visitors with one of these. Open daily 9:00–19:00, tel 431608, with offices at each train station as well.

Vienna has a fine, though complicated, transport system of buses, trams and subways. To simplify things (even though it probably won't pay for itself) buy the 72-hour pass for 92 AS (£4.15). I used it mostly to zip along the Ring. Get a transport map with your pass. Without a pass, blocks of 5 tickets at 13 AS (65p) each are cheaper than individual rides—18 AS (90p). Don't drive in Vienna. Ask at your hotel where to park your car and leave it there.

Food and accommodation
Vienna, like Munich, has plenty of rooms but nothing cheap. The T.I. room finding service will set you up for a 30 AS (£1.35) charge. Plan to spend £5.60 for a hostel bed or £19.50 for a small hotel double. Rooms in a private home are cheap (£5.60) but three days is the minimum stay and they are far from centrally located. In the summer, call one of these places a few days in advance.

Pension Columbia—Offering classy Old World elegance rare in this price range, friendly Herr Naschenweng speaks English and will hold a room until 17:00 with a phone call. A great value, 500 AS (£22.50) doubles, 630 AS (£28.50) triples, 760 AS (£34.35) quads, with shower. Kochgasse 9, 1080 Wien VIII, tel 426757, tram 5 from West Station, bus 13A from South Station.

Pension Lindenhoff—Lindenhofgasse 4, Vienna 1070, tel 930498. This place is clean and depressing, with good parking, very central location just off Mariahilferstrasse, 12 minutes walk from Hofburg, small breakfast, English spoken, 450 AS (£20.35) doubles.

Esterhazy Pension—Way out and clean but a very depressing entryway—a good example of not judging something by its cover. Also just off Mariahilferstrasse at Nelkengasse 3, Vienna 1060, tel 575159. Trams 52 and 58 take you straight from the Ring. No breakfast, English spoken, 450 AS (£20.35) doubles.

Pension Suzanne—This classy place is just across from the Opera at Walfischgasse 4, tel 5132507. More expensive with 710 AS (£32) doubles but nicer too. Call ahead.

International Studenthaus—This is a great value, actually within the Ring, 5 minutes from the Opera, a classy dorm offering 250 AS (£11.30) singles and 350 AS (£15.75) doubles (cheaper with hostel card or for longer stays). Open 1 July – 30 Sept, 170 beds but often full, call 5128463 between 8:00 and 11:00 to leave name. At Seilerstatte 30, Vienna A-1010.

Porsellaneum der Weiner Universitat—100 AS (£4.50) per person in singles and doubles, open July – Sept, at 9 Porzellangasse 30, between Ring and Franz Joseph Bahnhof, tram D, call 347282 first.

Youth Hostel Neubau—New, cheery, but normally full. B&B for 130 AS (£5.80), at Myrthengasse 7, tel 936316 or 939429.

The Viennese appreciate the fine points of life, and right up there with sex is eating. The city has many atmospheric restaurants. As you ponder the menus, remember Vienna's diverse empire may be gone but its flavour lingers. You'll find Slavic and Eastern European specialities here along with wonderful desserts and local wine. Three interesting drinks to try are Gruner Veltliner (green wine), Storm (very, very new wine, seasonal), and Traubenmost (a heavenly grape juice on the verge of wine, also seasonal, sometimes just called 'most'.

Here are some restaurants to consider:

Esterhazykeller—Self-service, rowdy, smokey, cheap, easy £2.25 meals, open 16:00 – 21:00, at 1 Haarhof near Am Hof, just off Naglergasse.

Augustinerkeller—Fun, like the Esterhazykeller, a bit touristy, two minutes from the Opera under the Albertina Museum at 1 Augustinerstrasse, open from 10:00 – 23:00.

Rathauskeller—Classy, in the city hall cellar, quite touristy with lots of tour groups, but still a good time and a good value. Live music after 19:00 in the Grinzingerkeller, closed Sundays.

12 Apostles—Most touristy of the 'kellers'—skip it.

Zo den 3 Hacken—Great goulash and atmosphere, at 1 Singerstrasse 28. Also check out the restaurant spilling onto the pavement one block away on Riemergasse.

Brezel Gwolb—A wonderfully atmospheric wine cellar with outdoor dining on a quiet square as well. Delicious inexpensive light meals, fine krautsuppe, even better for a late glass of wine. 1, Ledererhof 9, off Am Hof.

Zum Scherer Sitz u. Stehbeisl—Untouristy, in or outdoor, soothing woody atmosphere, intriguing decor, local specialities, good wine. At Judenplatz 7, near Am Hof, Mon – Sat 11:00 – 13:00, Sun 17:00 – 24:00.

Buffet Trzesniewski—Famous for its elegant and cheap finger sandwiches and small beers. Fun for a light lunch. Just off the Graben, across from Cafe Hawelka, 1 Dorotheergasse, Mon – Fri 9:00 – 19:30, Sat 9:00 – 13:00.

Naschmarkt—a cheap and good chain of cafeterias you'll find all over Vienna, £1.70 meals.

TOUR 10

VIENNA

Vienna is a head without a body. Built to rule the once grand
Hapsburg Empire—Europe's largest—she started and lost WWI,
and with it her far flung holdings. Today, you'll find a grand
capital ruling a relatively small and insignificant country.
Culturally, historically, and from a sightseeing point of view, this
city is right up there with Rome, Paris and London. With 1.6
million people, the town of Freud, Maria Theresa and Strauss
holds 20% of Austria's population. Last night we orientated
ourselves. Today we attack.

Suggested schedule	
9:00	Ride tram 1 for 360 degrees around the Ringstrasse, get off at City Hall and walk through Hofburg Gardens to the Opera.
10:30	City orientation tour. Leave it at Belvedere if you want to see 20th century art (Jugendstil).
12:00	Naschmarket, stroll, buy picnic, eat in Berggarten.
13:30	Neuburg museums and Hofburg.
15:00	Kunsthistorisches Museum.
17:00	Tram to Kursalon, Stadtpark. Concert behind Kursalon until 18:00.
19:00	Evening at the Prater amusement park or in old town.
Sleep	Vienna

Sightseeing highlights

● ● ● **Ringstrasse**—In the 1860s Emperor Francis Joseph had
the city's ingrown medieval wall torn down and replaced by a
grand boulevard 190 feet wide arcing 2½ miles around the city's
core. One of Europe's great streets, it's lined with diverse and
interesting architecture. Tram 1 circles the whole route and so
should you.

● ● **St Stephan's Cathedral**—Stephansdom is the Gothic
needle that the whole city spins around. With hundreds of years
of history carved in its walls and buried in its crypt (open
10:00–11:30, 14:00–16:30), this is a fascinating starting point for
a city walk. Tours of the church are German only, the 50-minute

daily mass is impressive, the crowded lift to the north tower
(daily 9:00 – 17:30) shows you a big bell but a bad view. If you
climb the 343 tightly wound steps of the spiral staircase to the
watchman's lookout, 246 feet above the postcard stand, you'll be
amply rewarded with Vienna's best view. From the top, orientate
yourself in the town, use your *A – Z* book to locate the famous
sights (open daily 9:00 – 17:00, March – Nov 15). The church is
nearly always open. The Stephansplatz around the square and the
nearby Graben ('ditch') street are colourful and lively.

●●● **Hofburg**—The complex, confusing and imposing Imperial
Palace demands your attention. Home of the Hapsburg emperors
until 1918 and still home of the Spanish Riding School, the
Vienna Boys' Choir, the Austrian president's office and several
important museums. Your *A – Z* sorts out this time-blackened,
jewel-stained mess nicely. While you could lose yourself in its
myriad halls and courtyards, after a strolling over-view I'd limit
your attention to three things:

The Imperial Apartments—These lavish Versailles-type rooms
are the ultimate in wish-I-were-God royal interiors. Open
Mon – Sat 8:30 – 1600, Sun 8:30 – 12:30, entrance from courtyard
under dome of St Michael's Gate. Must be seen with a tour and
tours are technically German only. Be sure that every eager wide-
eyed English-speaker in your group politely lets your guide know
you're dying to hear some English. This is a small town version
of the even grander Schonbrunn Palace. If you're rushed, skip
one or the other.

Treasury—The Weltliche and Geistliche Schatzkammer (secular
and religious treasure room) is one of the world's great collections
of historical jewels. Don't miss the 1000-year-old crown of the
Holy Roman Emperor.

The Neuburg, or new palace, is the last and most impressive
addition to the palace (from this century)—and newly opened to
visitors. Its grand façade arches around Heldenplatz. Check it out
quickly, not only to see its fine collection of weapons, musical
instruments, and classical statuary from ancient Ephesus, but to
wander among those royal halls, stairways, and painted ceilings.
Open Mon, Wed, Thurs and Fri 10:00 – 16:00, Sat and Sun
9:00—16:00, closed Tuesday.

●● **Opera**—The Staatsoper facing the Ring, just up from
Stephansdom and next to the T.I., is a central point for any
visitor. While the critical reception of the building 120 years ago
led the architect to commit suicide and it's been rebuilt since the
WWII bombings, it is a dazzling place and deserves a look. Tours
only, daily in English July and Aug at 10:00, 11:00, 13:00, 14:00,
15:00, other months, afternoons only, 25 AS (£1.15). The Vienna
State Opera, with the Vienna Philharmonic Orchestra in the pit,

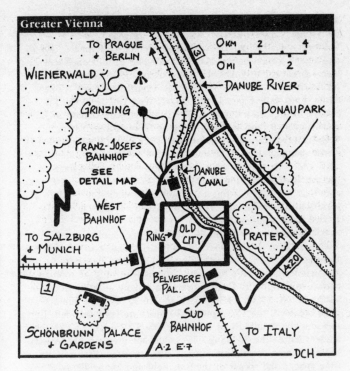

is one of the top three opera houses in the world. There are per-
formances almost nightly, except in July and August, with shows
normally sold out.

●●● **Museum of Fine Arts**—The Kunsthistorisches Museum
is the most exciting and varied collection of paintings on our
tour. Aside from a fine collection of Egyptian and Classical art,
and applied arts, including a divine golden salt shaker by Cellini,
you'll see the great Hapsburg Collection of masterpieces by the
likes of Durer, Rubens, Titian, Raphael, and especially Brueghel.
There are no tours or reasonable guidebooks but the paintings are
laid out on one easy floor and clear charts are posted to keep you
on course. Open Tues–Fri 10:00–18:00, Sat and Sun 9:00–18:00,
closed Monday. Picnic in the lovely park outside.

●● **Academy of Fine Arts**—Just three minutes from the
Opera, this small but exciting collection includes works by Bosch,
Botticelli, Rubens, a Venice series by Guardi, and a self-portrait
by 15-year-old Van Dyck. Schillerplatz 3, Tues, Thurs, Fri
10:00–14:00, Wed 10:00–13:00, 15:00–18:00, Sat and Sun
9:00–13:00, 15 AS (75p).

● **Albertina Collection of Graphic Arts**—Two minutes from
the Opera, this is a lovely collection of sketches by all the
masters. For a behind-the-scenes appreciation of Raphael, Durer
or Rubens, study their sketches. I was a bit disillusioned when I
learned that the originals are stored away and mostly copies are
on display—but it's still worthwhile. Augustinerstrasse 1, open
Mon, Tues, and Thurs 10:00 – 16:00, Wed 10:00 – 18:00, Fri
10:00 – 14:00, Sat and Sun 10:00 – 13:00, closed Sundays in July
and August. Rustic, fast and cheap cellar restaurant downstairs.

●**Belvedere Palace**—The elegant palace of Prince Eugene of
Savoy (conquerer of the Turks) houses the 'Austrian Gallery of
19th and 20th century art'. Skip the lower palace and focus on
the top floor of the upper palace (Oberes Belvedere) for a winning
view of the city and a fine collection of Jugendstil art—Klimt and
Kokoschka. Fine garden. Tues – Sun 10:00 – 16:00, entrance at
Prince Eugene Strasse 27.

●●● **Schonbrunn Palace**—The Schloss Schonbrunn is
Vienna's finest palace, is second only to Versailles in all of
Europe. Located far from the centre, it was the Hapsburg's
summer residence. It's big—1,441 rooms—but only 45 rooms are
shown to the public. English tours leave daily at 9:00, 10:00,
11:00, 12:00, 13:30, 14:30, 15:30 and 16:30. Sat and Sun are
most crowded; the 15:30 and 16:30 tours are least crowded. Entry
includes the required tour and is 50 AS (£2.25), 10 AS (50p) with
student card. The 30 AS (£1.35) guidebook gives an unnecessary
room by room description but is a nice souvenir. Pass any waiting
time around the corner in the four light and happy Bergyl
rooms—painted gaily for Maria Theresa by Bergyl (15 AS (75p)
including an interesting palace history exhibition). The sculpted
gardens and Gloriette Park are open till dusk, free, long walk to
Gloriette for nothing but a fine city view.

●● **Jugendstil**—Vienna gave birth to its own wonderful brand
of Art Nouveau around the turn of the century. It's becoming the
rage around Europe, and many come to Vienna solely in search of
Jugendstil. There are now city Judendstil walking tours (info at
T.I.) and the T.I. puts out a fine Jugendstil brochure. The best
of Vienna's scattered Jugendstil sights are in the Belvedere
collection, the Karlsplatz subway stop and the Clock on Hoher
Markt. The Museum of Applied Arts is disappointing.

● **City Park**—Vienna's Stadtpark is a gemutlichkeit world of
gardens, memorials to local musicians, ponds, peacocks, music in
bandstands, and local people escaping the city. Notice the
Jugendstil entrance at the Stadtpark subway station. The
Kursalon orchestra plays the Strauss waltzes daily from 16:00 to
18:00 and from 20:00 to 22:00. You can buy an expensive (£1.70
and up) cup of coffee for a front row seat or join the local senior

citizens and ants on the grass for a free fringe view.

● **Prater**—Vienna's sprawling amusement park tempts any visitor with its huge (220-foot high), famous but boring ferris wheel (Riesnrad), endless fun food places and rides like the rollercoaster, bumper cars and Lilliputian Railway. This is a fun and wacky place to share the evening with thousands of Viennese. For a family, local-style dinner eat at Wieselburger Bierinsel.

● **Nasch Market**—A typical old Vienna produce market bustles daily, just out from the Opera along Wienzeile Street. It's a bit seedy, surrounded by sausage stands, cafes and theatres, and each Saturday it sprouts a huge flea market.

●● **City Tours**—Of Vienna's many tours, I'd recommend the 'Getting Acquainted' tour that leaves daily from the Opera at 10:30, 11:45, 15:00 and, in the summer, 16:30. This 75-minute intro to the city covers a surprising amount of ground for 150 AS (£6.75). No reservations necessary, tel 7246830. Drop out of the tour at the Upper Belvedere if you'd like to see the art.

●● **Music**—Vienna is Europe's music capital but, sadly, in July and August the biggies are silent. The music season thrives from October to June, reaching a symphonic climax during the Vienna Festival each May and June. Normally the bigger halls attract the best talent. Even in the summer you'll find lots of top notch classical music. Try to take in a concert somewhere. The T.I. has ticket info.

● **Wine Gardens**—The 'Heurigen' is a uniquely Viennese institution celebrating (and drinking) the 'Heuriger', or new wine. Heurigen restaurants cluster at the edge of town doing their best to maintain their old village atmosphere and serve their homemade new wine with light meals and an enjoyable strolling-musicians type atmosphere. There are many Heurigen suburbs. Grinzing is the most famous and touristy. For a complete listing pick up the T.I.'s brochure. Newstift am Walde (bus 35A) is a local favourite with much of its original charm intact. (Try Haus Zimmermanns at Mitterwurzgasse 20, tel 441207.) Many locals say it takes several years of practice to distinguish between Heuriger and vinegar.

●● **The Viennese Coffee House**—The Viennese living room is down the street in a cosy coffee house. This tradition is just another example of the Viennese interest in good living. Vienna's many long-established (and sometimes even legendary) coffee houses, each with an individual character, offer newspapers, great pastries, sofas, elegance, and a take-all-the-time-you-want charm for the price of a cup of coffee. The coffee is very good and very strong. You may want to order 'brauner' (with a little milk) rather than 'Schwarzer' (black). Some of my favourites are: Cafe Hawelka (1, Dorotheergasse 6, closed Tuesday, just off the

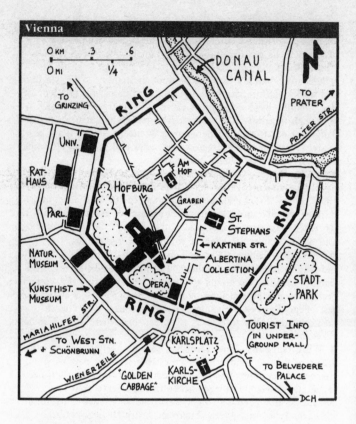

Graben) with a wonderful old 'brooding Trotsky' atmosphere, paintings on the walls by struggling artists who couldn't pay, a saloon wood flavour, chalkboard menu, smoked velvet couches, international selection of newspapers, and a phone that rings for regulars; the Central (1, Herrengasse 14, Jugendstil decor, great topfen strudle); the Sperl (6, Gumpendorfer 11, Jugendstil); and Cafe Ritter (6, Mariahilferstrasse 73, near recommended Esterhazy Pension) true, basic, stylish and interesting local crowd, no tourists, and the best smelling urinals in Europe.

Honourable mention—Several museums that try very hard but are submerged in the greatness of Vienna are: Historical Museum of the City of Vienna (Karlsplatz); Folkloric Museum of Austria (Laudongasse 15, 8th district); and the Museum of Military History (Heeresgeschichtliches, at 3, Arsenal, Objekt 18) probably Europe's best if you're into swords and shields.

TOUR 11

VIENNA TO THE TYROL

After some last minute sightseeing in Vienna we'll spend the early afternoon touring the magnificent Schonbrunn Palace and hit the autobahn for a non-stop 5-hour drive westward to the Tyrol. We'll spend the night in a small town just outside Innsbruck before carrying on into Switzerland tomorrow.

Suggested schedule	
9:00	Morning free, check out of hotel, possible other museums or browse downtown, St Stephans.
11:00	Opera tour.
12:00	Lunch at Augustiner Keller or picnic at Schonbrunn.
13:00	Drive to Schonbrunn, tour.
15:00	Hit the autobahn, 5 hour drive to near Innsbruck.
21:00	Arrive, Hall in Tyrol.
Sleep	Hall

Transport

To leave Vienna, drive along the gurtel to the West Bahnhof, turn right and follow the signs to Schloss Schonbrunn which is directly on the way to the West A-1 autobahn to Linz. There's plenty of parking at the palace. Leave by 15:00, beating the rush hour, following the autobahn signs to West A-1, passing Linz and Salzburg, nipping through Germany, turning right onto 93 in the direction of Kufstein and Austria at the Dreieck Inntal. Crossing back into Austria, you'll follow the scenic (but it'll be dark) Inn River Valley, stopping 6 miles east of Innsbruck at Hall in Tyrol. This 5-hour ride is non-stop autobahn all the way.

Those travelling by train should enjoy the rest of today in Vienna and catch the overnight train straight to Switzerland. There is a nightly 21:00 departure getting into Zurich at 8:30. Reserve a bed or couchette at the station when you arrive in Vienna.

Food and accommodation

The problem with today's plan is that we arrive late in a popular little town. Ideally, make a reservation over the phone. Halls' T.I.

is open 9:00 – 12:00 and 14:00 – 18:00, Sat till 12:00, closed
Sunday, tel 05223/6269. They can find you a room from a long
list of zimmers, pensions and gasthauses.

Gasthof Badl—This comfortable, friendly, big place run by the
Steiner family is very easy to find—immediately off the motorway
you'll see its lit sign (noise is no problem). At 350 AS (£16) for a
small double it's not cheap but take it for the convenience, the
big breakfast, and the fact that they'll hold a room for a phone
call. Innsbruck 4, A-6060, Hall in Tyrol, tel 05223/6784.

Since autobahn rest area food isn't great and you'll probably be
short on time, consider a picnic dinner for tonight. If you wait
till you arrive in Hall the kitchens may be closed.

TOUR 12

TYROL TO SWITZERLAND'S APPENZELL

After an easy morning in the town of Hall, a Tyrol mountain pleasure drive or a look at Innsbruck, we'll picnic at Innsbruck's Olympic ski jump and take to the autobahn for three Alpine hours to Switzerland's storybook friendly Appenzell to bask in the warm, intimate side of the land of staggering icy Alps.

Suggested schedule

8:00	Walk through Hall.
9:00	Drive into Innsbruck, see centre, tour museum, or skip Innsbruck and just drive, visit Olympic ski jump, picnic there.
12:00	Drive to Switzerland.
15:00	Altstatten, Gais, Stoss (viewpoint).
16:00	Set up in Appenzell, quick visit to Urnasch museum.
20:00	Appenzeller folk evening?
Sleep	Appenzell

SWITZERLAND

16,000 square miles. 6½ million people (400 per square mile, declining slightly). One Swiss franc = 38p; £1 = 2.65 SF.

Switzerland, Europe's richest, best-organised and most mountainous country, is an easy oasis and a breath of fresh Alpine air. Not unlike the Boy Scouts, the Swiss count cleanliness, neatness, punctuality, tolerance, independence, thrift and hard work as virtues. They love the awesome nature that surrounds them and are proud of their many achievements. The average Swiss income (second highest in the world), a great social security system and their super-strong currency, not to mention the Alps, give them plenty to be thankful for.

Switzerland, 60 per cent of which is rugged Alps, has distinct cultural regions and customs. Two thirds of the people speak German, 20 per cent French, 10 per cent Italian, and a small group of people in the southeast speak Romansh, a direct descendant of ancient Latin. Within these four language groups, there are many dialects. An interest in these regional distinctions will win the hearts of locals you meet. As you travel from one valley to the next, notice changes in architecture and customs (the

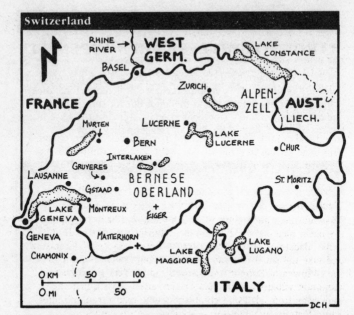

green Michelin guide is very helpful).

Historically, Switzerland is one of the oldest democracies. Born when three states, or cantons, united in 1291, the Confederation Helvetica as it was called (Roman name for the Swiss—notice "CH" on cars) grew to the 23 of today. The government is very decentralised and the canton is first on the Swiss citizen's list of loyalties.

Switzerland loves its neutrality, stayed out of both world wars, but is far from lax defensively. Every fit man serves in the army and stays in the reserve. Each house has a gun and a bomb shelter. Airstrips hide inside mountains behind Batmobile-type doors. With the push of a button, all road, rail and bridge entries to the country can be destroyed, changing Switzerland into a formidable mountain fortress. The USSR views Switzerland as a sort of 'Capitalist Alamo' and considers its 'armed neutrality' charming nonsense. August 1 is the very festive Swiss national holiday.

Switzerland has a low inflation rate and a very strong franc. Accommodation, petrol and groceries are reasonable, and hiking is free, but Alpine lifts and souvenirs are expensive. Shops throughout the land thrill tourists with carved, woven and clanging mountain knick-knacks, clocks, watches and Swiss army knives (Victorinox is the best brand).

The Swiss eat when we do and enjoy rather straightforward, no-nonsense cuisine: delicious fondue, rich chocolates, raclette, fresh dairy products (try Muesli yogurt), 100 varieties of cheese and Fendant, a surprisingly good local white wine. The Co-op and Migros grocery stores are the hungry hiker's best budget bet.

You can get anywhere quickly on Switzerland's fine road system (the world's most expensive to build per mile), or on its scenic and efficient trains. Tourist information offices abound. While Switzerland's booming big cities are quite cosmopolitan, the traditional culture lives on in the Alpine villages. Spend most of your time getting high in the Alps. On Sundays you're most likely to enjoy traditional sports, music, clothing and culture.

Transport

This morning, after a walk through Hall, you have two choices: a Tyrolean pleasure drive or a look at Innsbruck. If it's sunny, I'd drive. Backtrack on the motorway to Rattenberg (exit: Kramsach) and take the small riverside road 171 along the Inns through the pretty towns of Rattenberg, Schwaz and Volders. If you'd prefer mountain villages rather than a river valley, cross under the motorway from Hall and climb the scenic road through Tulfes, Rinn, Sistrans and Igls—great scenery . . . great names.

Just south of Innsbruck is the Olympic ski jump (signs say 'Bergisel'). Park here and climb to the empty grassy stands for a panoramic picnic before heading west on the autobahn to Landeck and Arlberg. The 8-mile long Arlberg tunnel saves you time but costs £5.60 and lots of scenery. For a scenic drive, skip the tunnel, exiting at St Anton, and lose 45 minutes going via Stuben.

For the rainy day city option to the pleasure drive, take the autobahn from Hall to the 'Innsbruck Ost' exit and follow the signs to the 'Stadtmitte' or 'Zentrum' and park as close to the old centre on the river as you can. There are city buses from Hall that'll get you there stress-free in 30 minutes.

After the Arlberg tunnel, you're just a few minutes from Switzerland. Leave the autobahn just after Feldkirch at Rankweil, taking the small road through Meiningen to Oberriet. As you cross the baby Rhine River, you leave Austria. From there it's an easy scenic drive following the signs through Altstatten and Gais to Appenzell.

By train, I'd streamline things by taking it overnight from Vienna to Luzern, spending the morning there, the afternoon in Ballenberg, and getting into the Interlaken region for dinner. Swiss trains are great and you'll have plenty of English-speaking help at each station.

Sightseeing highlights

● **Hall in Tyrol**—Take a lovely 'it's great to be alive' walk
through this easy-going town. From Gasthof Badl, walk over the
old pedestrian bridge into town. The first old building you'll see
is the Hasegg castle. Pick up a map and a list of town sights
here. Hall has a very colourful morning scene before the daily
tour buses arrive. The T.I. offers a daily 10:00 walking tour for
40 AS (£1.80) (in German unless several English-speakers are in
the group). They can give you driving instructions for Innsbruck
and info as well.

●● **Innsbruck**—After Salzburg and Vienna, Innsbruck isn't
much. If you do stop, the Golden Roof is the historic centre of
town. From this square you'll see a tourist information booth
with maps and lists of sights, the newly restored Baroque-style
Helblinghaus, the city tower (climb it for a great view) and the
new Olympics museum with exciting action videos for winter
sports lovers.

Nearby are the palace (Hofburg) and church and the very
important Tyroler Volkskunst Museum. This museum (60p, open
9:00–17:00 daily, closed Sunday afternoons) is the best look
anywhere at traditional Tyrolean lifestyles, with fascinating
exhibits ranging from wedding dresses and babies' cribs to
nativity scenes. Use the helpful English guidebook (£1.20).

A very popular mountain sports centre and home of the 1964
and 1976 Winter Olympics, Innsbruck is surrounded by 150
mountain lifts, 1,250 miles of trails and 250 hikers' huts. If it's
sunny, consider taking the lift right out of the city to the
mountaintops above.

●● **Side trip over Brennerpass into Italy?**—A short swing
into Italy is fast, easy and would give your trip an exciting new
twist (easy border crossing, no problem with car, Austrian
schillings accepted in the border region). To get there take the
great Europa Bridge over Brennerpass. It's expensive (about
£4.50) but in 30 minutes you'll be at the border. In Italy drive to
the colourful market town of Vipiteno Sterzing. Just south of
town, down a small road next to the autobahn, is the Reifenstein
Castle. The lady who lives there takes groups through on the
hour (with a break from 12:00–14:00) speaking German, Italian
and some English. It's a unique and wonderfully preserved
medieval castle. Tel 0472/65879.

● **Vorarlberg**—This westernmost corner of Austria has a special
style and charm. Both Feldkirch and Bregenz have well preserved
old quarters. For a great one hour walk, drive four miles out of
Dornbirn past Gutle to the Rappenlochschlucht gorge (walk from
the car park up to a peaceful lake and back through the
impressive river gorge).

Side trip through Liechtenstein?—If you must see the tiny country of Liechtenstein take this 30-minute detour: Feldkirch south on E77, drive through Schaan and Vaduz, the capital, cross the Rhine at Rotenboden and immediately get on the autobahn heading north from Sevelen to Oberriet.

●●● **Sightseeing in Appenzell**—Appenzell is Switzerland's most traditional region—and the butt of much local humour because of it. This is 'Landsgemeinde' country, where, until recently, entire villages would meet in town squares to vote. And vote meant men only. Even today, there are a few areas left where women can't vote on local issues. A gentle beauty blankets the region, overlooked by the 8,200-foot high peak, Santis. As you drive, you'll enjoy an ever-changing parade of finely carved chalets, traditional villages, and photogenic cows.

If you're here between 15 Aug and 15 Sept there's a good chance you'll get in on—or at least have your road blocked by— the ceremonial procession of flower-decked cows and whistling herders in traditional, formal outfits. The festive march down from the high pastures is a spontaneous move by the herding families, and when they finally do burst into town (a slow-motion Pamplona) everyone becomes a child, dropping everything and running into the streets.

After changing money in picturesque Altstatten, you'll wind up a steep mountain pass. Park at the summit where you see the tiny Stoss railway station. Cross to the chapel, walk through the meadow, open the electric wire gate and walk past the mellow munching cows to the monument which celebrates a local Appenzeller victory over Hapsburg Austria. From this spectacular spot you can see the Rhine Valley, Liechtenstein and the mountains of Vorarlberg back in Austria. This is an appropriate first stop in fiercely independent Switzerland. Enjoy the sun and the wind, stretch out on the stone for a snooze. This is a perfect picnic spot. Back by the chapel, the Wirtschaftz Stoss Inn is a rustic place for a drink or snack.

Now carry on through Gais and into Appenzell town. This is the most 'typical' town around and the best headquarters for the night. The T.I. is very good (8:00–12:00, 14:00–19:00, Sat 9:00–12:00, 14:00–16:00, closed Sun, tel 071-874111, on the main street, Hauptgasse 19). Ask about an Appenzeller folk evening. (Every night somewhere in town, about £1.70 without dinner.) Do your best to see one of these shows tonight. The little folk museum across the street is very good—unless you're going to its Urnasch equivalent.

Accommodation

Switzerland is more expensive than Austria and any time you get a double for less than £20 you're doing well. But it is also wonderfully organised—the phone system is easy, great T.I.s, English spoken regularly, and plenty of excellent youth hostels and dormitory-type alternatives to expensive hotels. If your budget is tight be sure to track down youth hostels (many with 'family rooms'—doubles) and keep your eyes peeled for matrazenlagers ('lager' means dormitory).

In Appenzell town the **Gasthaus Hof** offers by far the best cheap beds in town in its brand new matrazenlager. Dormitory beds cost 10 SF (£3.75), sheets 4 SF (£1.50), breakfast 4.50 SF (£1.70). Telephone in advance 071/872210, it's centrally located just off the Landsgemeindeplatz. The T.I. can set you up in zimmers for 20 SF (£7.50) per person with breakfast. The private homes at Sonnhalde (tel 873929) and Sonnenhalbstrasse 14 (tel 871765) are both good.

TOUR 13

APPENZELL TO THE BERNER OBERLAND

After a few short stops in cowbell country, we drive four hours (in Switzerland, 'drive' usually means 'scenic drive') to the Interlaken area, spending the afternoon at Switzerland's greatest open air folk museum, Ballenberg. After climbing through traditional houses from every corner of this diverse country and sampling the handicrafts and baking in action, we'll stop for a look at Interlaken before driving deep into the heart of the Alps, leaving our car and riding the gondola to the stop just this side of Heaven—Gimmelwald.

Suggested schedule

8:00	Pleasure drive through Appenzell, cheese tour in Stein.
10:00	Drive direct to Ballenberg, picnic en route.
14:00	Ballenberg museum.
17:00	Quick look at Brienzwiller, drive to Interlaken, 30 minute walk through Interlaken. Drive to Stechelberg for 18:55 lift.
19:00	Walter's Hotel, Mittaghorn, in Gimmelwald.
Sleep	Gimmelwald.

Transport

Head west out of Appenzell on the Urnasch road taking the first right (at the edge of town) to Stein. In Stein look for a big modern building and the Schankaserei sign. From there wind scenically south to Urnasch and down the small road to Wattwil. Drive through Ricken, Rapperswil, over the lake, and southward to Brunnen. From Brunnen, one of the busiest, most expensive to build and most impressive roads in Switzerland wings you along the Urnersee. It's dangerously scenic, so stop a few times at the many viewpoints to look. At Fluelen get on the autobahn for Luzern, vanishing into a long tunnel. Be careful to exit at Stans where a small road takes you along the Alpnachersee south toward Sarnen. Take the small chunk of autobahn, continue past Sarnensee to Brienzwiller before Brienz. A sign at Brienzwiller will direct you to the Ballenberg Openluft Museum. Park there. From Brienzwiller, drive along the congested north side of Lake Brienz. Take the blue, not green, exit sign into Interlaken. Turn right after the bridge and cruise through the old resort town

down its main street past the cow field and with great Eiger-
Jungfrau view on your left and T.I., post office, and banks on
your right. At the end of town you'll hit the West Bahnhof. Park
there. Allow 30 minutes to drive from Interlaken to the
Stechelberg cable-car car park. Head south toward Grindelwald
and Lauterbrunnen, pass through Lauterbrunnen town, noticing
the train station on your left and the funicular across the street
on your right, and drive to the head of the valley, a glacier-cut
cradle of Swissness, where you'll see the base of the
Schilthornbahn (a big grey cable-car station). This car park is safe
and free, ride the 18:55 lift (5 minutes, £1.70) to Gimmelwald. A
steep 100-yard climb brings you to the chalet marked simply
'Hotel'. This is Walter Mittler's Hotel Mittaghorn.

   Train travellers take the Luzern – Brunig – Brienzwiller train. At
the Brienzwiller station deposit your bag, note when later trains
depart for Interlaken, buy your Ballenberg ticket, and follow the
footpath into the museum. Carry on later by train to Interlaken-
Ost. Private trains go from the Interlaken-East station into the
Jungfrau region. Ask at the station about discount passes and
special fares. Spend some time in Interlaken before buying your
ticket to Lauterbrunnen. Take the train to Lauterbrunnen, cross
the street to catch the funicular up to Grutschalp where a special
scenic train rolls you along the cliff into Murren. From there
walk (45 min) downhill or ride the cable-car (£1.70 and a
100-yard uphill backtrack) to Hotel Mittaghorn. If you walk,
there's just one road leading out of Murren (marked with good
signs for Gimmelwald) and your hotel is the first building you
meet in Gimmelwald. Another option is to ride the post bus from
Lauterbrunnen to the base of the Stechelberg-Schilthorn cable-car
and ride up to Gimmelwald from there.

Sightseeing highlights

Stein—'The Appenzell Showcase Cheese Dairy' (Schankaserei) is
open daily from 8:00 – 14:00, audio-visual presentation and a look
at cheese ageing. It's fast, free and not very important—but they
do have cheap boxes of cold iced tea for sale (1 SF (38p)). The
T.I. and a new folk museum are right next door.

● **Urnasch**—An appealing one street town with my nomination
for Europe's prettiest museum. The Appenzeller Museum (on the
town square, open only from 14:00 – 17:00 daily, July – Oct, Wed,
Sat and Sun April – June, closed in winter, 3 SF (£1.15)) brings
this region's folk customs to life. Warm and homely, it's a pity it
doesn't work into our plan. (Consider a side trip from the
previous tour if you're early enough—it's an easy drive.) The
Gasthaus Oxchsen, three doors down from the museum, is a fine
traditional hotel (64 SF (£24) doubles) with good food and

wonderful atmosphere. Take a peek at the restaurant. Tel
071/581117.
● **Einsiedeln**—Just a few minutes off the road south of
Rapperswil is Switzerland's most important pilgrimage church.
It's worth a look if you're in the mood—like an Alpine Lourdes.
●●● **Ballenberg**—'The Swiss Open Air Museum Ballenberg' is
a rich collection of traditional and historic farmhouses from every
region of the country. Each house is carefully furnished and many
have a craftsperson working just as people did centuries ago. The
sprawling 50-acre park is a natural preserve and provides a
wonderful setting for this culture-on-a-spoon look at Switzerland.
Don't miss the Thurgau house (No.621) which has an interesting
wattle and daub display and an interesting bread museum
upstairs. Use the 2 SF (75p) map/guide. The more expensive
picture book is a better souvenir than guide. Open daily
9:30–17:30, 13 April–26 Oct, 7 SF (£2.65) entry, 2 hour private
tours are 45 SF (£17) (by prior arrangement), tel 0367/511123,
reasonable restaurant inside, and fresh baked or cooked goodies
available at several houses. Before leaving, drive through the little
wooden village of Brienzwiller, it's a museum itself.
● **Interlaken**—This is the original 19th century Alpine resort
when the Romantic movement redefined mountains as something
more than cold and troublesome obstacles. In fact, from that time
onwards, tourists have flocked to the Alps…'because they're
there'. Interlaken's glory days are long gone, its elegant old hotels
eclipsed by the new more jet-setty Alpine resorts. It is a good
administrative centre (good post office with boxes and long
distance phone booths, plenty of banks, major trains to all corners
of Europe) and shopping town, but I'd give it a once-over quickly
and head for the hills. By all means, sleep in the higher
villages—not here. T.I., on the main street, open Mon–Fri
8:00–12:00, 13:00–19:00, Sat 8:00–12:00, 13:30–17:00, Sun
16:00–18:00, tel 036/222121. Good info for the whole region.
Pick up Bern map, Jungfrau region map, and Jungfrau region
timetable.
● **Luzern**—Train travellers will probably pass through Luzern.
Near the station is the tourist office and the pleasant lakeside old
centre with its charming covered bridges—well worth a walk. The
sightseeing highlight of Luzern is undoubtedly its huge Museum
of Transport (Verkehrshaus des Schweiz) outside the town on the
lake (boats and cable cars go there from the centre). Europe's best
transport museum, it's open daily from 9:00 to 18:00 (Nov–Feb,
Mon to Sat 10:00 to 16:00), 10 SF (£3.75).

Food and accommodation
While Switzerland bustles, Gimmelwald sleeps. It has a youth

hostel, a pension and a hotel. The hostel is simple, less than clean, rowdy, cheap (non-members 12.50 SF (£4.75), members 5.50 SF (£2)), and very friendly. It's often full, so call ahead to Lena, the elderly woman who runs the place (tel 036-551704). The hostel has a self-service kitchen and is one block from the lift station. This relaxed hostel is struggling to survive. Please respect its rules, leave it cleaner than you found it, and treat it with loving care. Next door is the pension with rooms and meals. Up the hill is the treasure of Gimmelwald: Walter Mittler, the perfect Swiss gentleman, runs a chalet called **Hotel Mittaghorn.** It's a classic Alpine-style place with a million-pound view of the Jungfrau Alps. Walter is careful not to get too hectic or big and enjoys sensitive, back door travellers. He runs the hotel alone, keeping it simple but with class...He charges about £8 for bed and breakfast. (Address: 3826 Gimmelwald, Bern, Switzerland, tel 036-551658, English spoken.)

Other good budget beds in the region are at **Masenlager Stocki** (Lauterbrunnen, tel 551754), **Naturfreundehaus Alpenhof** (Stechelberg, 551202) and the **Chalet Schweizerheim Garni** (£12 per person in July and Aug, £8.50 off season, Wengen, 551581). Younger travellers love the cheap and American-orientated **Balmer's Herberge** in Interlaken (Haupstrasse 23, in Matten, tel 036-221961). There are two cheap 'lagers' at Kleine Scheidegg (25 SF (£9.50) for B&B, let the Interlaken T.I. telephone them for you) if you want to sleep in the clouds. A great budget bed in Lauterbrunnen is the **Schutzenbach Campground** run by Heinz and Christian von Allmen (most people in this valley are von Allmens). You'll see it on the left just past Lauterbrunnen toward Stechelberg. Open all year, 12 SF (£4.50)/person in 4- to 6-bed rooms, 10 SF (£3.75) in dorms, cheaper off season, must provide your own sheets, self-cooking facilities, tel 036/551268. If you get side-tracked in Brienz, its lakeside hostel (**Strandweg,** tel 036/511152, 10 SF (£3.75)) is great. And for something really different—almost weird—drive up the frighteningly narrow and winding Rosenlaui Valley road south from Meiringen (near Brienz) to the Hilton of the mountain climbers. At 4,000 feet altitude, in the middle of nowhere is the old world, tattered but elegant **Berg-Gasthaus Rosenlaui** (50 SF (£19)/double, tel 036/712912). At the head of that valley you can hike over Gross Scheidegg and down to Grindelwald. Nearby towns have plenty of budget accommodation. Let each village's tourist office help you out.

For dinner in Gimmelwald, ask Walter when you telephone him earlier, if he's cooking that night. Otherwise there's just the pension in the centre of the village. If you're at the hostel, bring some groceries and use the members' kitchen.

TOUR 14

FREE DAY IN THE ALPS

Today is your holiday from this all-go holiday. And a great place to recharge your tourist batteries is up here high in the Alps where distant avalanches, cowbells, the fluff of a down duvet and the crunchy footsteps of happy hikers are the dominant sounds.

If the weather's good we'll ride the lift from Gimmelwald to a classy breakfast at the 10,000-foot Schilthorn's revolving restaurant. Linger among Alpine whitecaps before riding or walking down to Murren and home to Gimmelwald.

Suggested schedule

None	You're on vacation!

Sightseeing highlights

Evening fun in Gimmelwald is found at the hostel (lots of young Alp-happy hikers and a good chance to share information on the surrounding mountains) and up at Walter's. Walter's bar is a local farmers' hangout. When they've made their hay, they come here to play. They look like what we'd call 'bumpkins' but they speak some English and can be fun to get to know. Walter knows how many beers they've had according to if they're talking, fighting, singing or sleeping. For less smoke and some powerful solitude, sit outside and watch the sun tuck the mountaintops into bed as the moon rises over the Jungfrau.

Helpful hints

Walter serves a great breakfast, but if the weather's good, skip his and eat atop the Schilthorn, at 10,000 feet, in a slowly revolving mountain-capping restaurant (of James Bond film fame). The early-bird special cable-car tickets (rides before 9:00) take you from Gimmelwald to the Schilthorn and back with a great continental breakfast on top for about £14. (Get tickets at the Station or from Walter.) Try the Birchermuesli-yogurt treat.

For hikers: The cable-car ride (Gimmelwald–Schilthorn–Gimmelwald) costs about £14. The hike (G–S–G) is free, if you don't mind a 5,000-foot altitude gain. I ride up and hike down or, for a less scary hike, go up and halfway down by cable car, then walk down from the Birg station. Lifts go twice an hour and the ride takes 30 minutes. (The round-trip excursion early-bird fare is

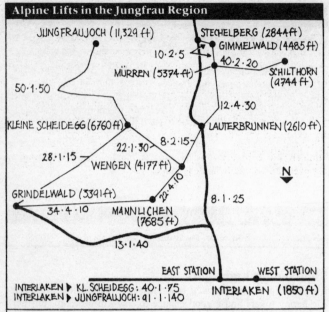

Alpine Lifts in the Jungfrau Region

JUNGFRAUJOCH (11,329 ft)   STECHELBERG (2844 ft)
                                    GIMMELWALD (4485 ft)
                    10·2·5   40·2·20
                MÜRREN (5374 ft)   SCHILTHORN
                                              (9744 ft)
50·1·50   12·4·30

KLEINE SCHEIDEGG (6760 ft)   LAUTERBRUNNEN (2610 ft)
            22·1·30   8·2·15
28·1·15   N
       WENGEN (4177 ft)
                          22·4·10
GRINDELWALD (3391 ft)   8·1·25
    34·4·10   MÄNNLICHEN
                (7685 ft)
          13·1·40

                    EAST STATION   WEST STATION
INTERLAKEN ▶ KL. SCHEIDEGG: 40·1·75
INTERLAKEN ▶ JUNGFRAUJOCH: 91·1·140   INTERLAKEN (1850 ft)

Code: Round-trip price in Swiss francs—Departures per hour—
Length of ride in minutes (e.g., 13-1-40 is 13 SF (£5) round-trip,
1 per hour, 40 minutes long).

Round trips are discounted only above towns (i.e. to Kl.
Scheidegg & Schilthorn). Buy one-way between towns for
flexibility. Maps, schedules and price lists are available at any
station. Lifts run from about 7 am to 8 pm. Groups of five or
more receive about a 20% discount. Discount Jungfraujoch trains
leave Kl. Scheidegg at 8:07, 9:07, 15:03, 16:00 and 17:10. Other
rides cost 16 SF (£6) more than price above. Stechelberg to
Gimmelwald: 25 & 55 past the hour, until 19:25.

cheaper than Gimmelwald – Schilthorn – Birg. If you buy the
ticket you can decide at Birg if you want to walk or ride down.)
Linger on top. Watch hang gliders set up, psych up and take off,
flying 30 or 40 minutes with the birds to distant Interlaken. Walk
along the ridge behind. You can even convince yourself you
climbed to that perch and feel pretty rugged. Think twice before
descending from the Schilthorn (weather can change, have good
shoes). Most people would have more fun walking down from
Birg. Just below Birg is a mountain hut. Drop in for soup, cocoa,

or a coffee-schnapps. You can spend the night for £2.80, tel 036/552640.

The most interesting trail from Murren to Gimmelwald is the high one via Gimmlin. Murren has plenty of shops, bakeries, tourist information, banks and a modern sports complex for rainy days.

Ask at the Schilthorn station for a souvenir badge or sticker. Gimmelwald is so undeveloped because it's classified 'avalanche zone'. It's one of the poorest places in Switzerland and many of the farmers, unable to make it in their disadvantaged trade, are subsidised by the government. Be careful not to confuse obscure Gimmelwald with very touristy and commercialised Grindelwald just over the Kleine Scheidegg ridge.

TOUR 15

BERNER OBERLAND HIKE AND ON TO LAKE GENEVA

This morning we'll enjoy the region's most exciting hike, making a loop up from Lauterbrunnen through Mannlichen, Kleine Scheidegg and Wengen. After lunch it's south into French-speaking Switzerland. With plenty of mountain beauty along the way we'll end the day in an entirely different mode touring the romantic Chateau Chillon on the edge of Lake Geneva.

Suggested schedule

7:30	Breakfast.
8:00	Lift to car, drive to Lauterbrunnen. Lift to Mannlichen (via Wengen), hike down to Wengen.
12:00	Lunch in Wengen, train to car.
13:00	Drive down Simmental, coffee at Taveyanne village.
16:00	Chateau Chillon.
17:00	Check into hotel or YH. Evening stroll along Montreux promenade.
Sleep	Montreux

Transport

If the weather's good leave Gimmelwald as early as possible. Park at the large multi-storey car park behind the Lauterbrunnen station, buy a ticket to Mannlichen and catch the train. Ride past great valley views to Wengen where you'll walk across town (don't waste time here if it's clear), buy a picnic if you like and catch the Mannlichen lift (departing every 15 minutes) to the top of the ridge high above you and spend the morning hiking back down.

From Lauterbrunnen head north catching the autobahn (direction Spiez, Thun, Bern) just before entering Interlaken. After Spiez turn left (direction Zweisimmen) into the Simmental Valley. After Saanen pass through the very rich and 'in' resort town of Gstaad (notice all the suits, ties and poodles—what a holiday!) and over the Col du Pillon pass. From here the most scenic route to Montreux forks left on the Villars road. Once you

hit the Rhone Valley take the small road, not the autobahn, to Lac Leman (Lake Geneva) and stop at the Chateau Chillon, parking on the road at the castle.

Train travellers will find trains leaving about every hour for the three-hour ride down Simmental to Montreux.

Sightseeing highlights

● ● ● **The Mannlichen – Kleine Scheidegg Hike**—This is my favourite Alpine hike, entertaining you all the way with glorious Eiger, Monch and Jungfrau views. From the top of the Mannlichen lift hike to the little peak for that 'king of the mountain' feeling. Then walk about an hour around to Kleine Scheidegg for a picnic or restaurant lunch. If you've got an extra £25 and the weather's perfect, ride the train through the Eiger to the towering Jungfraujoch and back. From Kleine Scheidegg, enjoy the everchanging Alpine panorama of the North Face of the Eiger, Jungfrau and Monch, probably accompanied by the valley-filling mellow sound of alp horns, as you hike gradually downhill (two hours) to the town of Wengen. If the weather turns bad or you run out of steam, you can catch the train earlier. The trail is very good and the hike is easy for any fit person. Wengen is a fine shopping town. Avoid the steep and boring final descent by catching the train from Wengen to Lauterbrunnen. (To check the weather before investing in a ticket, call 551022.)

● **Simmental**—The Simmen Valley ('tal' means valley) is
famous for its great milk cows. It's known locally for its fine
medieval churches (the most in the Berner Oberland) and for the
farmers who come to see the cows. The Erlenbach church (park
at the market square) is worth a look. The English brochure
explains that like most local churches, the beautiful paintings
decorating the interior were white-washed over in the 16th
century.

●● **Glacier des Diablerets**—For another grand Alpine trip to
the top of a 10,000-foot peak depart from Reusch or Col du
Pillon on the three-part lift. A quick trip takes about 90 minutes
and costs 32 SF (£12)—you could stay for lunch. From the top,
on a clear day, you can see the Matterhorn and even a bit of
Mont Blanc, Europe's highest mountain. This is your only good
chance to do or watch some summer skiing. Normally expensive
and a major headache to accomplish, it isn't bad here. Lift ticket,
hired skis, poles, boots and a heavy coat cost 30 SF (£11.50).
Since the slopes close at 14:00, you'd have to drive here direct
from Gimmelwald to manage.

●● Taveyanne—One of the most enchanting and remote villages
in Switzerland, Taveyanne is 2 miles off the main road between
Col de la Croix and Villars. A small sign will point you down a
small road on the left. It's just a jumble of log cabins and
snoozing cows stranded all alone at 5,000 feet. The only place in
town is the **Refuge de Taveyanne** where the Siebenthal family
serves hearty meals (great fondue and a delicious 'croute au
fromage avec oeuf' for 11.50 SF (£4.40)) in a prize-winning rustic
setting—no electricity, low ceilings, huge charred fireplace with a
cannibal-sized cauldron, prehistoric cash register, and well-hung
ornamental cowbells. This is French Switzerland and these people
speak nothing else. For a special experience consider sleeping in
their primitive loft—it's never full, 6 mattresses, access by a
ladder outside, 7 SF (£2.65), tel 025/681947.

●●● **Chateau Chillon**—This wonderfully preserved 13th
century castle set romantically at the edge of Lac Leman is a joy.
Follow the English brochure from one fascinating room to the
next—tingly views, a dank prison, weapons, interesting furniture
and even 700-year-old toilets. The long climb to the top of the
keep (No.25 in the brochure) isn't worth the time or sweat. Open
9:00–18:00 daily, 4 SF (£1.50), easy parking.

Food and accommodation

Resorty Lac Leman (Lake Geneva) is expensive. Call ahead, stay
inland, or prepare to spend. The perfect answer is the **'Haut
Lac' Youth Hostel** in the town of Territet (Passage de l'auberge

8, 1820 Territet). It's situated on the lake, a ten minute stroll north of Chateau Chillon, friendly, no traffic noise, English spoken, members only, any age, closed from 9:00–17:00, will hold a bed till 18:00 if you telephone (021/634934), 14 SF (£5.25) for sheets, bed and breakfast, 10 SF (£3.75) extra if you want the privacy of a double. Dinner at 18:30 for 8 SF (£3).

If you're not a hosteller try **Villa Tilda** (along the lake on Quai Vernex, tel 633814, 8 minutes from the station) or **Pension Wilhelm** (also near the station at Rue du Marche 13, tel 631431). Otherwise, Montreux's T.I. is open till 18:00 and if you telephone 021/631212 they'll tell you how much poorer you'll be by tomorrow morning (cheapest doubles normally 80 SF (£30)).

Itinerary options

Never overestimate the size of Switzerland. With its fine roads you could actually do everything in side-trips from a headquarters in the Interlaken district. Or you could see Chateau Chillon and drive up to Murten tonight.

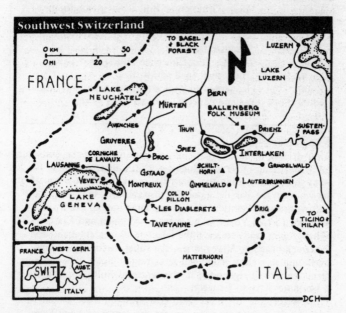

TOUR 16

THE HIGHLIGHTS OF FRENCH SWITZERLAND

After a look at Montreux and the Swiss Route du Vin we'll leave scenic Lac Leman to explore the fragrant home of Gruyere cheese, tour a chocolate factory, and settle in Switzerland's best-preserved walled town.

Suggested schedule

8:00	Check out of hotel, browse through Vevey market and waterfront.
9:00	Explore Corniche de Lavaux.
10:00	Drive to Gruyeres district.
11:00	Musee Gruerien in Bulle, buy picnic (both close at noon).
12:15	Picnic at Gruyeres town. Afterwards see cheese demonstration.
14:00	Tour Caillers Chocolate Fabrique in Broc.
15:30	Drive small road to Murten.
17:00	Get settled in Murten (or Avenches YH).
18:00	Explore Murten, ramparts, old town.
Sleep	Murten

Transport

After driving through Montreux and parking along the waterfront for a short stop in Vevey things get a little more complex. We want to continue along the lake past Vevey, not on the waterfront road nor on the parallel autobahn just above it, but along the narrow twisting Corniche de Lavaux for a tour of the Swiss vineyards. From Vevey follow signs to Mondon and Chexbres. When you're ready to leave the lake, get on the autobahn and backtrack nearly to Vevey where the super motorway swoops north and in a short while you're exiting at Bulle. The museum Gruerien is well signposted in the centre of Bulle. From there it's a 5-minute drive to Gruyeres.

Just before the 'driveway' into Gruyeres you'll see a modern 'cheeserie' on the right. Drop in for the demonstration. Then drive up the little road leading into the fortified traffic-free Gruyeres. Try to park in the second, closer car park. For the chocolate factory in Broc, five minutes away, follow the signs to 'Broc Fabrique' to the left just before the town square. If you're running out of film avoid the small road from Broc directly north to Fribourg—it's lined with picturesque houses and villages. Try to avoid driving in Fribourg (actually if you don't mind traffic, it's a fascinating town to spend a few miles just meandering around in). Signs to Bern will eventually lead you to signs to Murten.

Trains go regularly from Montreux through Lausanne to Fribourg where a tiny line will connect you to Murten.

Sightseeing highlights

● **Lac Leman (Lake Geneva)**—Separating France and Switzerland, surrounded by Alps, and lined with a collage of castles, towns, museums and vineyards, Lac Leman's crowds are understandable.

Boats carry its visitors comfortably to all sights of importance. The 11 SF (£4.20) ride from Lausanne to Chillon takes 90 minutes with stops in Vevey and Montreux (departing from Lausanne: 8:50, 10:50, 12:45, 14:00, 14:50 and 18:05, departing from the castle: 9:10, 12:29, 15:36, 16:23 and 17:19). Get the full story from any T.I. on the lake.

Montreux is an expensive resort with a famous jazz festival each July. Vevey nearby is a smaller and more comfortable resort town (Charlie Chaplin's last home). The Corniche de Lavaux is the Swiss Wine Road. Its picturesque towns, rugged winding roads and pretty vineyards attract and impress lots of tourists, producing most of Switzerland's tasty but expensive wine. Walkers can take the boat to Cully and explore on foot from there. Drivers can see it quickly and easily from their cars.

The most interesting city on the lake is Lausanne. You can park near its impressive cathedral and walk through the colourful old town. The Collection de l'Art Brut (at 11 Ave des Bergieres, open Tues–Fri 10:00–12:00, 14:00–18:00, Sat and Sun 14:00–18:00) is a fascinating and very thought-provoking collection of art by people who have been labelled criminal or crazy by our society.

●● **Musee Gruerien**—Somehow the unassuming little town of Bulle built a refreshing, cheery folk museum that teaches you all about life in these parts and leaves you feeling very good. It's small and easy, open Tues–Sat 10:00–12:00, 14:00–17:00, Sun 14:00–17:00, 4 SF (£1.50) and 1 SF (38p) for the excellent English guide. When it's over a sign reminds you 'The Golden Book of Visitors awaits your signature and comments. Don't you think this museum deserves another visit? Thank you!'

●● **Gruyeres**—This ultra-touristy town fills its fortified little hilltop like a bouquet. Its ramparts are a park and its ancient buildings serve the tourist crowds. The castle is mediocre and you

don't need to stay long, but make a short stop—it's a wonderful
setting. This is the home of Gruyere cheese and the modern
production centre in the valley at the foot of the town gives a
worthwhile (free and non-stop) look at how the cheese is made.
Open 6:00 – 18:00 daily. Cheese is actually being made from 9:00
to 11:30 and from 13:00 to 15:30. Hotels in town charge a
minimum of 80 SF (£30) per double.

● **Caillers Chocolate Factory**—The nearby town of Broc is
dominated by a huge chocolate factory. While you're in Switzerland it's fun to see how all the great chocolate is actually made.
This factory gives free one-hour tours with samples March – Oct
on Tues, Wed and Thurs from 9:00 to 10:15 and from 13:30 to
15:30. Closed in July. Tel 029/61212 to check.

● ● ● **Murten**—The finest medieval ramparts in Switzerland
surround the 4,600 people of Murten—or 'Morat' in French
(we're on the lingua-cusp of Switzerland here). The town has
three parallel streets, the middle one nicely arcaded, a mediocre
castle and city museum, a lovely setting overlooking the tiny
Murtensee and the rolling vineyards of gentle Mount Vully in the
distance. Try some Vully wine. The only required sightseeing is
to do the rampart ramble. The T.I., tel 037/715112, is very
friendly and has a handy town walk brochure.

● **Avenches**—This quiet little town, a few miles south of Murten,
was the capital of Helvetica—Roman Switzerland. Back then its
population was 50,000. Today it sleeps with the well-worn ruins
of the 15,000 seat Roman amphitheatre and an interesting Roman
museum.

Food and accommodation

An evening in Murten is so atmospheric that it's worth the
extravagance. The cheapest doubles in town rent for 60 SF
(£22.50). Try **Hotel Ringmauer** on Deutsche Kirchgasse near
the wall on the side farthest from the lake. Frau Gutknecht
charges 60 SF (£22.50) per double and runs a pleasant local-style
restaurant downstairs (tasty Rosti). Tel 037/711101.

The nearest **hostel** is a beauty—small, clean and laid back—in
Avenches at Rue du Lavoir 5, tel 037/752666, 14 SF (£5.25) or
19 SF (£7.20) in a double, open from 7:00 – 9:00 and from
17:00 – 22:00 as usual. Call ahead. This is the only budget
alternative to a hotel around, unless you want to struggle with
Bern tonight and go to its hostel (Weihergasse 4, down the stairs
from the parliament building on the river. Open daily 7:00 – 9:00,
17:00 – 24:00, lounge open all day, big, efficient, institutional, 8
SF (£3) 15 SF (£5.70) without a card, tel. 031/226316, 30 minute
drive from Murten).

TOUR 17

BERN TO THE BLACK FOREST

We'll spend most of the day in the Swiss capital city of Bern.
Stately but human, classy but fun, this is our best look at urban
Switzerland. Then we'll return to Germany, making a small town
in the legendary Black Forest home for the night.

Suggested schedule	
8:30	Drive to Bern.
9:00	Stop at Toblerone factory or go directly to Bern.
10:30	Park at Bern station, T.I. for info.
11:00	Tour Bundeshaus.
12:30	Lunch (consider river swim below Parliament).
14:30	Explore old town, shopping arcades, bear pits, view from rose garden.
16:30	Drive to Staufen.
19:00	Check into hotel.
Sleep	Staufen

Transport

Bern is just 30 minutes on the autobahn from Murten. If you
missed the chocolate at Broc, the impressive new Toblerone
factory overlooks the autobahn about five minutes outside Bern.
You'll see the factory on the right; take the Bernwohlen exit. As
you enter Bern follow signs to 'Zentrum' and 'Bahnhof'. When
you cross the bridge you're near the station. Park near the station
where you'll find the T.I. (If you picked up a Bern map in
Interlaken, remember to use it.) Leaving Bern, follow autobahn
signs for Zurich and Basel. Stay on E4 until you get to Basel
where Germany and France touch Switzerland.

Before Basel, you'll go through a tunnel and come to Reststatte
Pratteln Nord, a strange orange structure that looks like a huge
submarine laying eggs on the motorway. Stop here for a look
around one of Europe's greatest motorway stops. There's a bakery
and grocery store for picnickers, a restaurant and an exchange
desk open daily until 21:00 with rates 2% worse than banks.
Spend some time playing around, then carry on.

At Basel follow the signs to 'Deutschland' and then to
'Karlsruhe'. Once in Germany the autobahn will take you along
the French border which for now is the Rhine River. Exit at Bad
Krozingen, just before Freiburg, and cut down to Staufen. Park

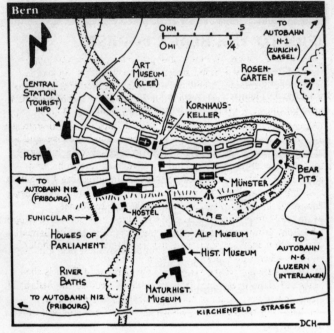

along the little river and you're just a bridge away from your hotel.

The bus or a milk train takes you into Bern where an hourly train takes you to Basel in 75 minutes. Train travellers should make their home base in Freiburg (in Germany, not to be confused with the Fribourg in Switzerland) and at least one train per hour makes the 40-minute Basel–Freiburg trip.

Orientation—Bern

If you must spend time in a big Swiss city, there's no doubt Bern's the one. The old town of Switzerland's capital fills a peninsula bounded by the River Aare. The main street (which changes its name several times) cuts the peninsula in half connecting the train station at the top with the popular 'bear pits', or 'Graben', over the bridge at the bottom. Trams run up and down this axis. (No.12 takes you from the pits back to the station.)

For a short well-organised visit: park your car at the station, visit the tourist office inside (open 8:00–20:30 daily, till 18:30 in winter, tel 03/227676, pick up map, list of museums and confirm your plans), follow the intro walking tour on the T.I. city map browsing your way downhill. Finish with a look at the 'Graben'

and a city view from the Rose Garden and catch a tram back up
to the station.

Sightseeing highlights
● ● ● **Old Town**—Window-shopping and people watching
through the lovely arcaded streets and busy market squares is
Bern's top attraction. The clock tower (zytgloggeturm) performs
at 4 minutes before each hour (tour its medieval mechanism daily
at 4:30, tickets 3 SF (£1.15) at T.I. or on the spot). The
Munster, or Cathedral, is worth a look. Climb the spiral staircase
100 yards above the town for a great view, good exercise, and a
chance to meet a live church watchman. Peter Probst lives way
up there watching over the church, answering questions, and
charging tourists for the view. Nearby is the imposing Parliament
building (Bundeshaus) of Switzerland (free, 45-minute tours most
days at 9:00, 10:00, 11:00, 14:00, 15:00 and 16:00, tel
031/618522 to confirm. Closed March, June and Sept, five people
minimum group size). Don't miss the view from the Parliament
terrace. You may see some national legislators but you wouldn't
know it—everything looks very casual.

● **Bear Pits** and **Rose Garden**—The symbol of Bern is the
bear, and some lively ones frolic their days away to the delight of
locals and tourists alike in the big barren concrete pits, or
'Graben'. Up the street is the Rosengarten. Worth the walk for
the great city view.

● **The Berner Swim**—For something to write home about, join
the local merchants, legislators, publishers and students in a
lunchtime float down the Aare River. The Bernese, proud of their
very clean river and their basic ruddiness, have a tradition—sort
of a wet, urban paseo—of walking upstream 15 to 30 minutes and
floating playfully or relaxed back down to the excellent (and free)
riverside baths and pools (Aarebad) just below the Parliament
building. If the river is a bit much, you're welcome to enjoy just
the Aarebad.

● ● **Museum of Fine Arts (Kunstmuseum)**—Located 4 streets
from the station, it features 1,000 years of local art and some
Impressionism, but the real hit is its fabulous collection of Paul
Klee paintings. If you don't know Klee, I'd love to introduce
you. Open Wed–Sun 10:00–17:00, Tues 10:00–21:00.

Other Bern Museums—Across the bridge from the Parliament
building on Helvetiaplatz are several museums (Alpine, Berner
History, Postal) that sound more interesting than they are. Albert
Einstein's House is an interesting stop in the town centre on the
main street.

● ● **Toblerone Chocolate Factory**—The Suchard-Tobler
Company has opened a huge new factory and it proudly offers

visitors a film, a mouth-watering English tour through seas of
molten chocolate and vats of samples. It's a very impressive
place—especially if you like Toblerone. Tours are Tues, Wed and
Thurs at 9:00 and 13:30, Mon at 13:30 only, closed July and
Oct, tel 031/343511 to confirm plans.

● **Staufen in Breisgau**—This is a pretty ('pretty' is the
standard Black Forest adjective) town in the Black Forest. It's a
mini-Freiburg—a perfect combination of smallness and off-the-
beaten-pathness with a quiet pedestrian zone of colourful old
buildings bounded by a happy creek which actually babbles.
There's nothing to do here but enjoy the marketplace atmosphere
in the morning. Walk through the vineyards to the ruined castle
overlooking the town and savour a good dinner with local wine.

Food and accommodation
The Black Forest has lots of hotels and enough visitors often to
fill them. It's wise to call ahead. Staufen makes a good overnight
stop. The T.I. (Mon – Fri 8:00 – 16:30, Thurs till 18:00, Sat
9:00 – 11:00, Sunday closed, tel. 07633/80536) has room lists and
can help.

Try to stay at **Hotel Kreuz Post.** It's friendly, immaculate, has
lots of character, pretty rooms, good food, right in the pedestrian
zone just over the bridge. Hauptstrasse 65, 7813 Staufen/Breisgau,
tel 07633/5240, closed Wed at 14:00 until Friday morning, 47
DM (£15) per double.

Hotel Sonne is also in the centre, classier and more expensive,
75 DM (£24) per double, tel 07633/7012.

Gasthaus Bahnhof is colourful in a ruddy way. This is the
cheapest place in town, across from the very sleepy station, castle
behind, no breakfast, self-cooking facilities, a little depressing. 20
DM (£6.50) per person. Tel 07633/6190.

Gasthaus Rossle in the hamlet of St Ulrich, 15 minutes
north-east of Staufen, is my rural choice. In a woody typical
Schwarzwald setting, with fine beds and great food, a very
traditional local-style place, only locals. 24 DM (£7.60) per
person, tel 07633/252. Drive on to the end of the road for the
view and a walk.

Train travellers may choose to sleep in Freiburg. The T.I., two
blocks in front of the station, tel 0761/216, can find you a 60
DM (£19) double. The big, modern **hostel** is at the edge of town
at Kartauserstrasse 151, tram 1 to Romerhof, tel 0761/67656, 14
DM (£4.50).

TOUR 18

THE BLACK FOREST—SCHWARZWALD

We'll spend the day exploring the best of this most romantic of German forests. By late afternoon we'll be settled in Germany's greatest 19th century spa resort and ready for a stroll through its elegant streets and casino, finishing the day with a 'Kur'—sauna, massage and utter restfulness.

Suggested schedule

8:00	Stroll Staufen.
9:00	Freiburg, park near tourist office. Enjoy pedestrian zone, Munster Platz, Augustina Museum, buy picnic.
11:30	Drive into Black Forest, picnic at or near St Peter.
14:00	Drive north to Baden-Baden.
15:00	Baden-Baden, get settled, browse through elegant town centre.
17:00	Take the Kur.
20:00	Dine in the city centre.
22:00	Stroll Lichtentaler Alley.
Sleep	Baden-Baden

Transport

From Staufen drive to Freiburg, parking near the T.I. or station (signs 'Bahnhof'). The centre of town is a pedestrian zone circled by a ring road with lots of parking. Leave Freiburg on Schwarz-waldstrasse which becomes scenic 31 down Hallental toward Titisee. Turn left at Hinterzarten onto road 500 turning later to drive through the towns of St Margen and St Peter. From St Peter take the winding Kandelhof road to Waldkirch where a fast road will take you to the 'Freiburg Nord' autobahn entrance and you'll take the autobahn north towards Karlsruhe and Baden-Baden. Follow the autobahn into Baden-Baden. If you're heading for the youth hostel turn left at the first light after the motorway ends, and follow the signs winding uphill to the big modern hostel next to a public swimming pool. Otherwise drive straight into town until you see the T.I. signs near a fountain-filled park.

Train travellers will need to simplify. After probably sleeping in Freiburg let the T.I. recommend the most scenic public transport route to get to Baden-Baden (hourly 90-minute rides). Consider

the Schauinsland excursion and the Freiburg—Baden-Baden train.
The 'Baden-Oos' station is 5 miles from the centre. Take bus 1
or 3 to Augustaplatz. (Hostellers get off long before the centre at
Grosse Dollen Strasse.)

Orientation
The Black Forest, or Schwarzwald, is impressively Catholic and
traditional. On any Sunday you'll find 'folk marches', traditional
costumes, and a particularly heavy load of local colour. It's a
range of hills stretching north—south along the French border
from Karlsruhe to Switzerland. It's so thickly wooded the people
called it black. Today it's popular for its clean air, cheery
villages, hiking possibilities and cuckoo clocks.

While many parts are layered with commercialism, our
proposed route fills your day with intriguing looks at local life
and lots of Schwarzwald beauty.

Sightseeing highlights
● ● **Freiburg**—This 'sunniest town in Germany' with 180,000
people, 22,000 students, university town vibrancy, French and
Austrian history, bombed and rebuilt since WWII, is the 'capital'
of the Schwarzwald. It's pleasant, but nothing to telephone home
about. Enjoy its pedestrian-only old centre. Freiburg's trademark
is its system of 'Bachle' or tiny streams running down each street.
Very fresh and clean today, but imagine back 500 years when
these were the town's sewer system. Absorb the ambience of ice
cream and street singers on the cathedral, or Munster, square.
The actual church with a towering tower (not worth the 116
metre ascent) is impressive. Don't miss the Augustiner Museum
for a fine look at local culture and a great close-up look at some
of the Munster's medieval stained glass downstairs. (Open
10:00–17:00, Wed 10:00–20:00, all of Freiburg's museums are
free.)

The T.I. (between old centre and station, tel 0761/261) has a
fine 3 DM (95p) city guidebook, room-finding service, and info
on the entire Black Forest region. Bounce your plan for the day
off these people. They offer daily guided walks.

● **Schauinsland**—Freiburg's 'own mountain' is the handiest
quick look at the Schwarzwald for those carless ones (it was
designed for Freiburgers relying on public transport). At its 4,000
foot summit there is a 'panorama restaurant', pleasant circular
walks, a tower on a nearby peak offering a commanding Black
Forest view, and the Schniederli—a 1592 farmhouse museum. Ask
at the T.I. for the package rate from Freiburg. 14 DM (£4.50)
will get you there and back including the town centre-to-lift tram
ride. The Schauinsland cable car is one of Germany's oldest.

● **Badenweiler**—An idyllic but poodle-elegant and finicky-clean spa town known only to the wealthy Germans who soak there; if ever a town was a park, Badenweiler is it. Next to the ruins of a Roman mineral bath in a park of imported and exotic trees (including a California redwood) is the Markgrafen-bad (bath). This prize-winning piece of architecture perfectly mixes the trees and peace with an elegant indoor-outdoor swimming pool. It's open to the public (Mon, Wed, Fri 8:00−20:00, Tues, Thurs and Sat 8:00−18:00, Sun 9:00−18:00, 9 DM (£2.85)). The locker procedure is quite different and the language barrier may nearly sink you. Towels, caps and suits can be hired. For a sauna: men—Mon 17:00−21:00, women—Wed 17:00−21:00, mixed sauna (nude) on Fridays 17:00−21:00, 10 DM (£3.20). My wife and I happened in on a Friday evening and had no choice but to get comfortable with a handful of naked German strangers and one Frenchman who comes over every week. 'Travel as a temporary European' is what I always say!

●● **The Scenic Black Forest Drive**—This pleasant loop from Freiburg takes you through the most representative chunk of the area, avoiding the touristy and over-crowded Titisee. Stop whenever you can to enjoy the clean 'healthy' air that doctors actually prescribe for people from all over Germany. A good walking centre is the town of St Peter. Its T.I., just next to the fine church, open Mon−Fri 7:30−12:00, 13:30−17:00, can recommend a walk. Without any long stops, this route will get you from Freiburg to Baden-Baden in three hours.

●●● Baden-Baden—Of all the high class resort towns I've seen, Baden-Baden is the easiest to enjoy on a budget in jeans. 150 years ago this was *the* playground of Europe's elite with the world's top casino. Royalty and aristocracy would come from all corners to 'take the Kur'—soak in the curative (or at least they feel that way) mineral waters. Today this town of 50,000 attracts a more middle class crowd and serves as a great homebase for northern Black Forest explorations. Baden-Baden has a tremendous tourist office complete with lounge and library (right in the centre near the riverside park at Augustaplatz 8, Mon−Sat 9:00−22:00, Sun 10:00−22:00, tel 07221-275200).

The best approach to Baden-Baden, given our tight schedule, is to arrive by 16:00 and spend one hour just browsing through the centre enjoying ritzy window displays, gardens, street fairs and fountains. After taking a 'Kur' at 17:00, dine at 20:00 and finish the evening bestowing upon yourself a royal title and promenading down the famous Lichtentaler Alley. (This is lit at night. During the day consider taking the city bus to Koisterplatz and walking its entire length back into town.)

Tomorrow morning, even if you don't gamble, tour the casino.

It's open for gambling from 14:00 – 6:00 (5 DM (£1.60) entry, 10 DM (£3.20) minimum bet, tie and coat required) but gives dicey tours of its Versailles-rivalling interior every morning from 9:30 to 12:00 (2 DM (65p) and no ties!)

The Germans who come to Baden-Baden generally stay put for two weeks and the T.I. has enough recommended walks and organised excursions to keep even the most energetic holidaymakers happy.

● ● ● **The Roman-Irish Bath**—The highlight of most Baden-Baden visits is a sober two-hour ritual called the Roman-Irish Bath. Friedrichsbad, on Romerplatz 1, pampered the rich and famous in its elegant surroundings when it opened 150 years ago. Today this steamy world of marble, brass columns, tropical tiles, herons, lily pads, and graceful nudity welcomes gawky tourists as well as locals.

For 25 DM (£8) you get the works. The routine is explained in the English brochure and on the walls, following the red arrows. You'll probably get lost about halfway through but don't worry— linger in the various thermal baths and saunas until you're melted and don't miss the cold plunge. You'll get a key, locker and towels. The attendants are used to clumsy tourists and speak enough English. Youth hostelers can pick up a 5 DM (£1.60) discount coupon at the hostel. Open Mon 8:00 – 22:00, Tues 8:00 – 16:00, Wed 8:00 – 16:00 and 16:00 – 22:00 mixed, Sat 8:00 – 12:00, and 12:00 – 22:00 mixed, Sun closed. The nearby more modern Caracalla baths are open Sundays. The dress code is always nude. 'Mixed' means men and women together.

Afterwards, browse through the special exhibits and Roman artifacts in the gallery, sip just a little terrible but 'magic' water from the elegant fountain, and stroll down the broad royal stairway feeling, as they say, 'five years younger',—or at least no older.

Accommodation

Except for its hostel, rooms in Baden-Baden are fairly expensive. But the T.I. can always find you a room if you arrive by 17:00. Private zimmers require longer stays. Take advantage of Baden-Baden's great new **Werner Dietz Youth Hostel** at Hardbergstrasse 34, bus 1 or 3 to Grosse Dollenstrasse, tel 07221/52223, open 8:00 – 23:30, always saves 30 beds to be doled out to 'travellers' at 17:00, 16 DM (£5) including sheets, extra in a double room, overflow hall when all beds are taken, 5 DM (£1.60) discount coupons for bath, good meals.

TOUR 19

BADEN-BADEN TO THE MOSEL VALLEY

After touring one of the world's most lavish casinos, we'll leave Baden-Baden for a look at Germany's oldest town, Roman Trier, and an afternoon meandering through the village vineyards and soothing views of the Mosel River Valley.

Suggested schedule	
9:30	Tour Baden-Baden casino.
11:00	Drive to Trier with possible stop in Heidelberg or Trier.
15:00	Mosey up the Mosel Valley.
17:00	Find zimmer in Zell.
Sleep	Zell am Mosel

Transport

From Baden-Baden there's no direct road to Trier. Your fastest and easiest bet is to remember that in Germany the shortest distance between any two points is the autobahn, and cut past Karlsruhe, Ludwigshafen and Kaiserslautern. From Trier follow the signs to the Mosel Valley letting the scenic riverside route 53 wind you north past Bernkastel-Kues to Zell am Mosel.

Those travelling by train should rearrange things a bit, taking the express to Koblenz (Baden-Baden to Koblenz, changing in Mannheim, two per hour, two-hour ride) and a train down the Mosel to Trier (hourly, 75-minute rides) or skipping Trier and setting up in Cochem (on the Trier line).

Sightseeing highlights

Heidelberg—This famous old university town attracts hordes of tourists and any former charm is stained almost beyond recognition by commercialism. If you must see it don't let yourself—you've seen much better on this trip.

Speyer—You'll be going right by it—and if you'd like to see Germany's most impressive Romanesque cathedral, drop in.

●● **Trier**—Germany's oldest city lies at the head of the scenic Mosel Valley, near the border of Luxembourg. Founded by Augustus in 15 BC, it was 80,000 strong when Constantine's father used the town as the capital of the fading Western Roman Empire. A short stop here offers you a look at Germany's oldest Christian church and its oldest Gothic church (Dom and Liebfrau churches, open 6:00−20:00 and 14:00−17:30). Also, you'll find

Karl Marx's house (fascinating to Marx fans, 15 minute film at 20 past each hour, Tues – Sun 10:00 – 18:00, Mon 13:00 – 18:00).

Trier has a lovely park featuring the remains of a Roman bath and the striking 4th century relics of the Roman Emperor's summer residence now built into a palace and church. The famous and huge Porta Nigra (best Roman fortifications in Germany, climb to the top) is noteworthy, but skip the city museum in the adjacent courtyard. The Hauptmarkt square is a pleasant swirl of fruit stands, flowers, painted facades and fountains—with a handy public w.c. Trier's tourist office next to the Porta Nigra is open Mon – Sat 9:00 – 18:00, Sun 9:00 – 13:00, tel 0651/75440; when closed a coin-operated machine dispenses maps and room lists.

● ● ● **Mosel Valley**—The Mosel is what many visitors hoped the Rhine would be—peaceful, sleepy, romantic, with fine wine, plenty of castles and hospitable little towns with lots of zimmers. Boat, train and car traffic here is a trickle compared to the roaring Rhine. While the Mosel flows from France to Koblenz where it flows into the Rhine, the most scenic piece of the valley lies between the towns of Bernkastel-Kues and Cochem. I'd savour only this section.

Bernkastel, while pretty, is overrated and overcrowded, but the vine-draped castle-studded hills and the meandering Mosel north of there are lovely. The town of Zell am Mosel is best for an overnight stop—peaceful, with a fine riverside promenade, a pedestrian bridge over the river and plenty of zimmers, colourful shops, restaurants and weinstubes.

Further downstream, Beilstein is the quaintest of all Mosel towns. Check out its narrow lanes, ancient wine cellar and ruined castle.

Cochem, with its majestic castle and picturesque medieval streets, is the tourist hub of this part of the river. Even with its tourist crowds, it's worth a stop. The Cochem castle is spectacular—even if it's the work of over-imaginative 19th century restorers (15 March – 15 Nov 9:00 – 17:00, tours on the hour, 3 DM (95p)). Consider a boat ride from Cochem to Beilstein (1 hour) or to Zell (3 hours).

Berg Eltz is my favourite castle—possibly in all of Europe. Set in a mysterious forest, left intact for 700 years, furnished throughout as it was 500 years ago, it's a must (April – Oct, Mon – Sat 9:00 – 17:30, Sun 10:00 – 17:30, 4.50 DM (£1.50), by train walk from Moselkern station, midway between Cochem and Koblenz).

Train travellers have some interesting transport options along the river. While the train can take you along much of the river, consider riding the KD line (Koln – Dusseldorf) which sails from

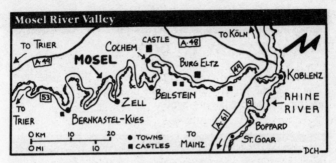

Trier to Bernkastel-Kues and from Cochem to Koblenz. You can
also hire bikes at some stations, leaving them at others, or hire a
bike from Zenz at Enderstrasse 3 in Cochem. If you find yourself
stranded in some town, hitching isn't bad.

Throughout the region on summer weekends, you'll find wine
festivals with oom-pah bands, dancing, colourful costumes and
lots of good food and wine. Any local T.I. can give you a
schedule.

Accommodation

Zell is my choice for the evening. The tourist office (next to the
Rathaus) posts room vacancies even after it closes. During my
August visit, 80% of the town's zimmers had beds available. Try
the home of Fritz Mesenich—quiet, friendly, clean, central, across
from a good weinstube, 25 DM (£8) singles, 40 DM (£12.70)
doubles with breakfast (as usual), Oberstrasse 3, 5583 Zell/Mosel,
tel 06542/4753.

For a cosier town farther north, sleep in one of Beilstein's many
zimmers. The T.I. (02673/1417, or 7912 in the winter) is open
daily from 7:00–19:00 in the Cafe Klapperburg.

If you yearn for the closest thing around to a big city, sleep in
Cochem. It has plenty of zimmers on Oberbachstrasse and
Endertstrasse and a youth hostel over the bridge and left half a
mile down Bergstrasse (02671/8633, 9 DM (£2.85)). The Cochem
T.I. (tel 02671/3971, open Mon–Thurs 8:00–17:30, Fri
8:00–19:00, Sat and Sun 10:00–13:00, 14:00–17:00) books
rooms, too.

TOUR 20

MOSEL VALLEY TO BONN

After touring the town of Cochem and the great Eltz Castle, we'll
travel up to the Rhine and over to the home of West Germany's
government and Beethoven—Bonn.

Suggested schedule	
9:00	Cochem, skip castle, buy picnic.
10:30	Berg Eltz, picnic after tour.
13:30	Drive rest of Mosel, taking the autobahn from Koblenz to Bonn.
16:00	Park near station, visit T.I., get set up. Evening free.
Sleep	Bonn

Transport

You can't get lost if you stick to the river. For Berg Eltz drive to
the car park at the end of the road above Moselkern, or if you'd
like to skip the enchanting but long 30-minute walk to the castle,
drive around through Lasserg and Wierscheim. The quickest way
to Bonn is to enter the autobahn where it crosses the Mosel
(Koblenz-Dieblich) and head north following the signs to Koln
and Bonn. For a look at Koblenz, Remagen and the capital
buildings in Bonn-Bad Godesberg, follow the Mosel into Koblenz,
work your way to the Deutsches-Ecke where the rivers touch,
then leave town on highway 9 along the Rhine through Mulheim,
Andernach, and Remagen.

In Bonn, take the 'Bonn-Endenich' exit and follow signs to
'Zentrum', 'Stadt-mitte,' 'Bahnhof' and T.I. Park near the
Bahnhof, there's a big car park just north on Thomasstrasse.

By train simply change in Koblenz, catching one of many
expresses to Bonn and Koln. (Don't get off in Bonn-Bad
Godesberg.)

Sightseeing highlights

Koblenz—Not a nice city, but its historic Deutsches Eck (German corner), the tip of land where the Mosel joins the Rhine, has
a certain magnetism. (Koblenz means 'confluence' in Latin—the
town has Roman origins.) Walk through the park, notice the
blackened base of what was once a huge memorial to the Kaiser.
Across the river, the yellow fortress is now a youth hostel with all
the comfort of a WWI trench.

Remagen—Just to the north are the remains of the 'Bridge at Remagen' of World War II fame. Not much remains but the memorial and the bridge stubs are enough to stir the emotions of any who remember when it was the only remaining bridge that allowed the Allies to cross the Rhine and race to Berlin in 1945. Never closed. Just follow the signs, it's a small town.

Bonn-Bad Godesberg—This suburb of Bonn is the home of West Germany's government. Very little is open to the public, but as you're driving into Bonn on highway 9, you'll go right by the parks, monuments, embassies and important buildings that make up a national capital.

●● **Bonn**—Bonn was chosen as West Germany's temporary capital after WWII when German unity was still on the cards. Its sleepy, peaceful nature seemed like a good place to plant Germany's first post-Hitler government. Today it is sleek, modern, and by big city standards, remarkably pleasant and easy going. We're stopping here not to see Beethoven's house or the parliament buildings (neither are very interesting) but to come up for a breath of the real world before finishing off this tour on the misty romantic Rhine.

The T.I., directly in front of the station, is excellent (8:00 – 21:00, Sun 9:30 – 12:30, tel 0228/773466, free room finding service). Stop here for info, to confirm tomorrow's plans, and to get advice on overnight parking.

The market square and Munsterplatz are a joy as is the local shopping and people-watching.

Accommodation

Hotels are expensive in Bonn but the T.I. is very helpful, and— unlike just about anywhere else we've been—July and August are the least crowded months, since the government takes a summer break.

Of great value is the **Hotel Eschweiler,** perfectly located just off the market square on a pedestrian street next to Beethoven's place (ten-minute walk from the station—don't drive). The family that owns and runs the place charges 60 DM (£19) for a double (70 DM (£22.25) with a shower), speaks English, and keeps a parakeet in the breakfast room. Bonngasse 7,5300 Bonn 1, tel 0228-635385.

TOUR 21

BONN, KOLN AND THE RHINELAND

Today we get a good dose of no-nonsense urban German muscle,
visit its greatest Gothic cathedral along with one of its finest art
museums and drive back into the fairytale world of Rhine legends
and castles.

Suggested schedule

9:00	Catch boat to Koln, see cathedral and museums, and take the train back to Bonn.
13:00	Lunch, afternoon free in Bonn.
16:00	Drive south to Bacharach.
Sleep	Bacharach

Transport

Big city driving is something most normal people try to minimise.
Today we can avoid it entirely by taking the boat up to Koln and
returning by train (or vice versa, train ride—7 DM (£2.25), 4 per
hour, 20-minute ride. Ask at the T.I. for boat schedules. All the
important sights in each town are within comfortable walking
distance between the train and boat stations. Plan this upon
arrival in Bonn at the T.I.). If you decide to drive to Koln, park
in the car park under the cathedral.

From Bonn catch the autobahn south (direction Frankfurt),
getting off in Koblenz and following the highway 9 signs in the
direction of Mainz. ('Umleitung' is a common road sign around
here; it means 'detour'.) Highway 9 will put you right on the
Rhine's west bank. Now the castle fun begins.

Train travellers should take the train from Bonn through
Koblenz to Boppard, a good place to catch one of the KD boats.
If you're rushed, stay on the train to whatever Rhine village you
choose to call home. Express trains don't stop in small towns so
you'll probably be changing trains in Koblenz. The walk from the
Koblenz Bahnhof to the boat dock is much longer than in the
smaller towns further south.

Sightseeing highlights

● ● **Koln (Cologne)**—This big no-nonsense city—Germany's
fourth largest—has a tight and fascinating centre. Since the Rhine
was the northern boundary of the Roman Empire, Koln, like
most of these towns, goes back 2,000 years. It was an important
cultural and religious centre throughout the Middle Ages. Even

after WWII bombs destroyed 95% of the city, it remains, after a
remarkable recovery, a cultural and commercial centre as well as a
fun and colourful city.

Its Dom, or cathedral, is far and away Germany's most exciting
Gothic church. 50 yards from the station, tours Mon – Fri at
10:00, 11:00, 13:30, 15:30, and 14:30, Sat at 10:00 and 11:00.
Next to the Dom is the outstanding Romisch-Germanisches
Museum, this tour's best Roman museum (Tues – Sun
10:00 – 17:00, Wed and Thurs till 20:00, you can view its prize
piece, a fine mosaic floor, free, from the front window). Sadly,
the displays are in German only. The Wallrof-Richartz Museum
has a fine new home between the Roman museum and the river.
If you like modern and pop art, don't miss it (Tues – Sun
10:00 – 17:00, Tues and Thurs 10:00 – 20:00, tel 0221/2212379).
The T.I. near the station, opposite the Dom's main entrance, is
very helpful—tel 0221/2213345, daily 8:00 – 22:30.

Charlemagne's Capital, Open Air Folk Life, and **Phantasialand**—If you have an extra day, a number of interesting sights are
within easy striking distance of Bonn and Koln. Aachen is a very
historic town—the capital of Europe in 800 AD, when Charles
the Great called it Aix-la-Chapelle. The remains of his rule are
there including a very impressive Byzantine/Ravenna-inspired
church with his sarcophagus and throne. The city also has a top-
class newspaper museum and great fountains including a clever
arrange-'em-yourself version.

If you'd like to learn more about regional folklife, visit the
Rheinisches Freilichtmuseum (open air museum) in a lovely
natural setting near Kommern (take the Euskirchen – Wisskirchen
autobahn exit southwest of Bonn).

And if you'd like to fight the lowbrow local crowds at a second-
rate local Disneyland, visit Phantasialand. It's popular enough to
have its very own autobahn exit south of Bruhl between Bonn
and Koln.

Food and accommodation

Where to stay on the Rhine is a wonderful problem. There are so
many fine choices. Every town has plenty of zimmers and
gasthauses offering beds for 20 to 25 DM (£6.50 to £8) per
person. For cheaper beds there are several special youth hostels.
And each town has a helpful T.I. eager to assist you. Finding a
room should be easy any time of year. St Goar, Bacharach and
Oberwesel are the best towns for an overnight stop.

In St Goar I stay one mile north of town in the friendly riverside **Hotel Landsknecht** (tel 06741/1693). Klaus Nickenig and
family offer doubles for 75 DM (£23.75) and a classy Rhine
terrace. In town, and easier for those without transport, is **Hotel**

Montag (Heerstrasse 128, just across the street from the world's largest free hanging cuckoo clock, tel 1629, all new rooms, 80 DM (£25.50) doubles). Mannfred Montag and his family speak English and run a good shop (especially for steins) adjacent. The best 25 DM (£8) hotel beds in town are at **Gasthof Stadt St Goar** (Pumpengasse 5, tel 1646, near station) and **Gasthof Weingut Muhlenschenke** (actually a small winery with tasting for 6 DM (£1.90)), your best cosy out-of-town bed (Grundelbach 73, tel 1698, 27 DM (£8.50) per person). St Goar's best **zimmers** are the homes of Frau Wolters (Schlosberg 24, tel 1695, on the road to the castle, great view, cosy, 20 DM (£6.50)), Frau Kurz (Ulmenhof 11, tel 459, 2 minutes from the station, 24 DM (£7.70)), and Frau Schwarz (Heerstrasse 86, tel 7585, very central, on the river, only one room, call first, very very homely, almost too homely, 20 DM (£6.50)). The St Goar **hostel** is a big white building under the castle, run very Germanically, and is good value with beds for £2.80 and good dinners £2.25, tel 06741/388.

The town of Bacharach, near St Goar, has Germany's best youth hostel—a castle on the hilltop with a royal Rhine view. **Jugendherberg Stahleck,** closed from 9:00 – 17:00, members of all ages welcome, 12.50 DM (£4) per bed, normally places available in July and Aug, tel 06743-1266, ten-minute climb on trail from town church or drive up. These **zimmers** are central, charge about 20 DM (£6.50) and speak some English: the homes of: Gerturd Aman (Oberstrasse 13, tel 1271), Annelie Dettmar (Oberstrasse 18, tel 2979), Kathe Jost (Blucherstrasse 33 tel 1717), Christel Ketzer (Blucherstrasse 51, tel 1617). My choice for the best combination of comfort, hotel privacy with zimmer warmth, central location and medieval atmosphere, is the friendly **Hotel Kranenturm** run by Kurt and Fatima Engel. This is actually part of the medieval fortification, and former towers are now round rooms. Located near the railway lines (ask Kurt to explain his special windows to you) at Langstrasse 30, tel 06743/1308. Great cooking and a Kranenturm ice cream special that may ruin you. 25 DM (£8)/person. For atmospheric dining elsewhere in Bacharach try the **Altes Haus,** the oldest building in town.

Oberwesel, an underrated town with a wine fest during the second week of September, has a friendly T.I. (tel 06744-8131) and a super modern **Youth Hostel** behind the castle, a 20-minute walk from town. (They speak English and will hold rooms, tel 06744/8355, pool, 4, 2 and 1-bedrooms 11 DM – 22 DM (£3.50–£7), good meals.) **Hotel Goldener Pfropfenzieher** (Am Plan 1, tel 207) is old, creaky and hotelish with doubles costing 60 DM (£19) and up. A good zimmer is the home of **Anni Rheinbay** at Liebfrauchstrasse 42, friendly, central, great value at 20 DM (£6.50)/person.

TOUR 22

THE RHINE AND ITS CASTLES
FLY HOME FROM FRANKFURT

A fitting finale for this tour is a day on the Romantic Rhine.
We'll cruise the most exciting stretch and climb through the
Rhineland's greatest castle before returning, if necessary, to the
Frankfurt airport to catch our flight home.

Suggested schedule	
9:00	Boat to St Goar, explore Rheinfels Castle, buy picnic.
12:00	Boat back to Bacharach.
13:00	Picnic in park. Afternoon free.
	Return to Frankfurt, return car and fly home.

Transport

Today's tempo is dictated by your post-tour plans. If your flight
leaves after 15:00 you can easily take the cruise and tour the
castle. If it leaves earlier, do the cruise and castle on Tour 21.
And, if you can spend another night here, this can be a leisurely
day. Train travellers will find handy overnight trains leaving
Frankfurt for Berlin, Copenhagen, Paris or London.

Rather than get bogged down with times, I'll just explain
general possibilities. While trains stop about hourly even in the
small towns, zipping travellers north or south, the most enjoyable
way to experience the valley is on a KD steamer. These run in
both directions several times a day stopping at nearly every
village. Koblenz to Bingen costs 41 DM (£13) Boppard to
Bacharach is 20 DM (£6.50). Groups of 15 get a 20% discount.
Reservations are never necessary but always call or ask locally to
confirm your plans. Taking the boat one way and returning by
train is logical. Trains leave major towns almost hourly, and rides
are very quick (St Goar–Bacharach 12 min., Bacharach–Mainz
30 min., Mainz–Frankfurt 30 min.). There's a lovely cycle path
down the river, but contrary to some sources, you can't hire bikes
at stations. While there are no bridges between Koblenz and
Mainz, several small ferries do the job nicely.

If you are rushed, the speediest schedule is: tour Rheinfels
castle from 9:00 to 10:00, cruise from St Goar to Bacharach from
10:15 to 11:20, picnic in Bacharach and catch the 12:42 train to
Frankfurt arriving at 14:05.

Sightseeing highlights along the Rhine (working south from Koblenz).

Stoltzenfelds Castle—Just south of Koblenz past the huge brewery you'll see this yellow castle. It's a steep 10-minute climb from the mini car park directly below, for a great castle interior. Open 9:00 – 13:00, 14:00 – 18:00, closed Mondays.

Marksburg—Across the river from the village of Spey, you'll see the best preserved castle on the Rhine, Marksburg. It has a mandatory tour in German only and they've put the castle on the wrong side of the river. It makes an exciting photograph, though.

● **Boppard**—Worth a stop. Park near the centre (or at the DB train station and walk). Just above the market square are the remains of a Roman wall (we've seen better). On the square, buy the little Mainz – Koblenz guidebook (4.50 DM (£1.50)) with a map. This describes every castle and town we'll see.

●● **Rheinfels Castle**—This mightiest of Rhine castles is an intriguing ruin today. Follow the castle map with English instructions (50 pf (15p) at the ticket window) through the castle. If you follow the castle's perimeter, circling behind, you'll find a few of the several miles of spooky tunnels—explore. (A flashlight would be handy.) Be sure to see the reconstruction of the castle in the museum to see how much bigger it was before Louis XIV destroyed it. The castle shop sells an excellent children's book called 'Father Rhine Tells His Sagas'—the big edition, 10 DM (£3.20), has great pictures. Open daily 9:00 – 18:00, ten minutes' steep walk up from St. Goar.

St Goar—A pleasant town with good shops (steins and cuckoo clocks, of course), waterfront park and a helpful T.I.

Loreley—This big rock—the ultimate Rhine-stone—is famous for its legendary nymph who used to distract sailors causing them to run aground. (Occasionally, if you listen very carefully, you can still hear her.) Any postcard rack will tell you the complete story. This is actually the narrowest part of the Rhine, and a nearby reef makes things even more exciting. There's nothing on the rock except a German flag.

● **Bacharach**—Just a very pleasant old town that misses most of the tourist glitter. Next to the KD dock is a great park for a picnic. Herr Kruger in the T.I. is insistently helpful (open Mon – Fri 8:00 – 12:30, 13:30 – 17:00, tel 06743/1297, follow signs through a courtyard and up stairs). Some of the Rhine's best wine is from this town.

Mainz, Wiesbaden, and **Rudesheim**—Are all too big, too famous, and not worth your time. Mainz's Gutenburg Museum is also a big disappointment. For a note on Frankfurt, look back under Tour 1.

Best of the Rhine

Departure procedure

If you're flying home from Frankfurt be sure to telephone your airline three days in advance to conform your seat. Also, call the morning of your departure to check the departure time.

To get to the airport by autobahn, head toward Frankfurt. After you cross the Rhine, follow signs to 'Flughafen'. The airport ('Flughafen') is right on the autobahn and there are plenty of signs to direct you.

By train it's even easier. Take the train to the Frankfurt central station and follow the signs again to 'Flughafen'. There's an airport shuttle train every ten minutes and you'll be there in twelve.

POST-TOUR OPTION

BERLIN

No tour of Germany is complete without a look at its historic
capital—Berlin. And it's not included! My greatest frustration in
putting this plan together was my inability to work Berlin in. If
you have a couple of extra days, take the easy overnight train ride
from Frankfurt and experience the soul of old Germany and the
pain of modern Germany.

Suggested schedule

Day 1

7:00	Arrive (overnight trains arrive early), at Berlin's Zoo Bahnhof station.
8:00	Stop by T.I., get room, move in.
9:00	K'dam—visit Memorial church, tour Ka-De-We Department store, buy picnic.
11:30	Picnic on grounds of Charlottenburg Schloss.
12:00	Tour Palace, cross the street for museum, see Nefertiti.
15:00	Dahlem Museum complex, tour gallery.
17:00	Back to hotel to rest, or relax at Wannsee, take a cruise?
19:00	Dinner (Turkish?) near Savignyplatz or on K'dam.
21:00	Sample Berlin nightlife (or watch it) on K'dam.

Day 2

8:00	Breakfast, consider checking out of hotel, store luggage at station.
9:00	Stroll through Tiergarten, climb Siegessaule for good E & W view, visit Reichstag History Museum. (Consider hour walk along from Brandenburg to Charlie via Potsdamer Platz.)
11:00	Haus am Checkpoint Charlie Museum.
12:30	Walk over wall, Checkpoint Charlie, stand-up lunch near Unter den Linden.
14:00	Museuminsel—Pergamon Museum.
16:00	Explore people's centre—Palast der Republic.
17:00	Changing of guard at Monument to Victims, eternal flame (unless Wed., 14:30).
17:30	Museum of German History.
19:00	Stroll Unter den Linden to Brandenburg Gate.
20:00	Dinner at fast food stand near Fernsehturm.
21:00	Cross back to west, subway to Bahnhof to catch westbound train.

Getting there

The government subsidises flights into Berlin (PanAm, British Airways and Air France charge as little as £30 from several German cities) and driving in a simple matter of buying a 6 DM (£1.90) transit visa at the border and taking the autobahn straight through East Germany, but I'd recommend the overnight train in and out from and to Frankfurt at the end of your trip after turning in your hire car.

The night train from Frankfurt (22:35 to 6:13) costs 157 DM (£50) round trip second class plus 23 DM (£7.50) for the sleeper (couchette). Buy it round trip with reservations as soon as you are sure of the dates (i.e. in Munich). Your East German transit visa is issued free on the train.

Berlin sightseeing

Kurfurstendamm—The glitter of the crazy 20s echoes here, and pampered by economic subsidies from the west, this thriving Champs-Elysees of Germany is a great place to feel the pulse of Berlin—capitalist and determined to be western, K'dam is the heart of the new West Berlin. At the head of K'dam is the main station, Europa Center, Kaiser Wilhelm memorial church and Savignyplatz.

Kaiser-Wilhelm Gedachtniskirche (memorial church)—This most important WWII memorial, with charred and gutted ruins of the old bombed out church, has great ceiling mosaics. Next to it is the very impressive new church. Go inside for a world of blue glass. You'll see why they call this complex the broken tooth, lipstick and the powder compact.

Schloss Charlottenburg—This is the only surviving Hohenzollern Palace and Berlin's top baroque palace. Open Tues–Sun, 9:00–16:00 (bus 54 from Zoo, mandatory tours, in German only) in a pleasant royal garden. Across the street is the Egyptian Museum worth a wander if only to look into the eyes of the elegant 3,000-year-old bust of Queen Nefertiti, from the days of King Tut.

Dahlem Museum—Actually a cluster of important museums which those with an unending appetite for art and culture could spend an entire trip in. Seven museums, all free and open Tues–Sun, 9:00–17:00, bus 1, 10, or 68 or U-Bahn to Dahlem-Dorf. Most important is the Gemaldegalerie (Picture Gallery) with over 600 canvases by Durer, Titian, Botticelli, Rubens, Vermeer, Bruegel, and the world's greatest collection of Rembrandts including the 'fake' but lovely 'Man with the Golden Helmet'.

The Reichstag—The old parliament building, burned by Hitler to frame the communists, now houses a fine modern Germany history exhibit. History buffs will enjoy comparing this with the perspective from the left shown in East Berlin's counterpart. Nearby is the historic Brandenburg Gate and a good view of the wall. Open 10:00 – 17:00, Tues – Sun, free. Take bus 69 from Zoo, the only English film is at 14:00 daily.

The Wall—This 100 mile border erected almost overnight by East Germany (and friends) in 1961 is thirteen feet high with a sixteen foot tank ditch and one hundred and sixty feet of no man's land. The opposite of a medieval rampart, this keeps people in. Once called the Anti-Fascist Protective Rampart by the East, still called disgusting by most in the West, this wall defines Berlin today—and is a fascinating tourist sight. View it from a platform on the desolate Potsdamer Platz (the former Piccadilly Circus of Berlin), mid-way on a grey and eerie walk from Brandenburg Gate to Checkpoint Charlie.

Don't miss the fascinating Haus am Checkpoint Charlie, the little museum that tells the history of the wall, imaginative escape attempts and all. (U-Bahn to Kochstrasse, just before you cross at Checkpoint Charlie, open daily 9:00 – 22:00.)

Honourable mention sights:

Zoo— The world's largest (and possibly the best) zoo stretches out from Berlin's central station. (9:00 – 17:00, entrance fee, feeding times posted at entry, morning is the best visiting time.) Next to the zoo is Berlin's biggest and most pleasant city park, the 'Tiergarten'.

Gedenksstatte Plotzensee Memorial—Powerful memorial to Nazi victims in Hitler's former execution chambers.

Bauhaus Archiv-Museum—Popular with architects and fans of modern design.

Siegessaule—Memorial tower, climb its 285 steps for a good view of East and West.

TOURIST INFORMATION (T.I.)

Each of these countries has an excellent network of tourist information offices both locally and in the UK. Before your trip, send a letter to each country's National Tourist Office (listed below) telling them of your general plans and asking for info. They'll send you the general packet and if you ask for specifics (calendars of local festivals, good hikes around Fussen, castle hotels along the Rhine, the wines of Austria, etc.) you'll get an impressive amount of help. If you have a specific problem they are a good source of help.

During your trip your first stop in each town should be the tourist office where you'll take your turn at the informational punching bag smiling behind the desk. This person is rushed and tends to be robotic. Prepare. Have a list of questions and a proposed plan to double check with him or her. They have a wealth of material that the average 'Um, do you have a map?' tourist never taps. I have listed phone numbers throughout, and if you'll be arriving late, or want to arrange a room, call ahead.

The great frustration for us English-speakers is touring great sights with a German-only guided tour. It's much more work for a guide to struggle in English and most don't want to. The most famous sights normally have English tours when 20 or so people gather, or they hand out read-along fliers. Be sure to let your guide know politely but firmly that several people here speak only English and are dying to know more about this place. Then stare hungrily at the guide until a little English info sneaks out as the rest of the group enters behind you or leaves the room.

National Tourist Offices in the UK:

Austrian National Tourist Office
30 St George Street, London W1R 0AL (tel 01-629 0461)

German National Tourist Office
Nightingale House, 65 Curzon Street, London W1Y 7PE (tel 01-734 2600)

Swiss National Tourist Office
Swiss Centre, New Coventry Street, London W1V 8EE (tel 01-734 1921)

TRANSPORT

DRIVING

This route is ideal by car. Every long stretch is autobahn
(motorway) and nearly every scenic backcountry drive is paved
and comfortable. Drivers over 21 need only their UK licence and
the insurance that comes automatically with your hire car;
though acquiring the Green Card is also advisable. There are no
border formalities to worry about.

The local rules of the road are much like ours. Learn the
universal road signs (charts explain them in most road atlases and
at service stations). Seatbelts are required and two beers under
those belts is enough to land you in gaol.

Use local maps and study them before each drive. Familiarise
yourself with which exits you need to look out for, which major
cities you'll travel in the direction of, where the ruined castles
lurk, etc. Pick up the 'cardboard clock' (available free at petrol
stations, police stations and Tabak shops) and display your arrival
time on the dashboard so parking attendants can see you've been
there less than the posted maximum stay (blue lines indicate
90-minute zones on Austrian streets).

To understand the complex but super-efficient autobahn (no
speed limit, toll free) pick up the 'Autobahn Service' booklet at
any autobahn service area (free, listing all intersection signs,
stops, services, etc). Use a good map, study the intersection
signs—'dreiecke' means three corners or a 'y' in the road,
'autobahn-kreuz' is a 'cross' or an intersection. Petrol stations are
spaced about every 30 miles, normally with a restaurant, small
shop, and sometimes a tourist info desk. Exits are often 20 miles
apart. Know what you're looking for—nord, sud, ost, west or
mittel—miss it and you'll be long gone. When driving slower than
120 mph, stay out of the left hand passing lane. Remember, in
Europe, the shortest distance beween any two points is the
autobahn. Signs directing you to the autobahn are usually green.

Try to hire a car with a boot so you can leave 'deep storage'
things safely out of sight. I keep a box in the boot for things I
don't need to cart in and out of hotels. My picnic hamper sits on
the back seat and I equip it for easy and enjoyable, time-and-
money-saving car picnics (either at the very pleasant autobahn
picnic areas or as I drive—if my navigator can play cook). I stock
up with plenty of orange juice in litre boxes, paper towels, plastic
cups, and so on. Copy the car key as soon as possible for safety
and so that two people can have access to the car.

BY TRAIN

Germany, Switzerland, and Austria By Train	
Day	Overnight In:
1	Arrive Frankfurt, train to Rothenburg — Rothenburg
2	Sightsee Rothenburg, afternoon Romantic Road bus to Munich — Munich
3	All day Munich — Munich
4	All day Munich, side trip to Dachau — Munich
5	Tour highlights of Bavaria, Mad Ludwig's Castle — Reutte
6	Tyrol, Berchtesgaden, Salzburg — Salzburg
7	Salzburg with side trip into Salzkammergut — Salzburg
8	Early train to Melk, tour abbey, cruise Danube — Vienna
9	All day in Vienna — Vienna
10	All day in Vienna — Night Train
11	Tour Luzern, Ballenberg Folk Museum — Near Interlaken
12	Hike Grindelwald-Kl. Scheidegg-Lauterbrunnen — Gimmelwald
13	Free day to relax in Alps — Gimmelwald
14	Travel to Montreux, Chateau Chillon — Montreux
15	Cruise Lake, visit Lausanne, Murten — Murten
16	Sightsee Bern, into Black Forest — Freiburg
17	Freiburg, Black Forest or Baden-Baden — Freiburg or Baden-Baden
18	Express Train to Cochem via Mannheim and Cochem — Koblenz
19	Explore Mosel, Berg Eltz, set up in Bonn — Bonn
20	Bonn, Koln, set up in Rhineland — Bacharach
21	Cruise Rhine, tour Rheinfels castle — Bacharach
22	Fly home from Frankfurt —

While this itinerary is designed for car travel, it can be adapted
for train and bus. The trains cover all the cities very well but can
be frustrating in several rural sections.

If you are under 26 this itinerary would make the purchase of
an Inter-Rail ticket allowing unlimited travel on most European
trains worthwhile, especially if you are travelling alone. Tickets
are available from authorised travel agents and main British Rail
ticket offices and cost £145. They are valid for a month.
Alternatively substantial discounts are available through
Transalpino and BIGE.

If you are over 26 or decide to buy tickets as you go, look into
local specials. Seniors (women over 60, men over 65) and youths
can enjoy substantial discounts.

Each segment of this plan is explained for rail travellers in the
main text. For more information take advantage of the very
helpful train station information offices. Tell them what you want
to do and they'll tell you how to do it by rail or bus.

A train/bus version of this trip requires some tailoring to avoid
areas that are difficult without your own transport and to take
advantage of certain bonuses that train travel offers. Trains in this
region are punctual and well organised.

EATING AND DRINKING

The local cuisine is heavy and hearty. While it's tasty, it can get monotonous if you fall into the schnitzel or wurst and potatoes rut. To eat well, use a phrase book and be adventurous. Each region has its local specialities which, while not the cheapest, are often the best values on the menu.

There are many kinds of restaurants. Hotels often serve fine food. A 'Gaststatte' is a simple, less expensive resturant.The various regions' many ethnic restaurants provide a welcome break from the basic Germanic fare. Foreign food is either from the remnants of a crumbled empire (Hungarian and Bohemian—where Austria gets its goulash and dumplings) or a new arrival to serve the many hungry but poor guest workers. Italian, Turkish, Greek and Yugoslavian food in Germany and Switzerland is commonplace and good value. Chinese food and 'new cuisine' from France and Italy are more and more popular. The cheapest meals are found in department store cafeterias, 'Schnell-Imbiss' (fast food) stand-up places, university cafeterias (called 'mensas',—tourists welcome) and at youth hostels.

Most restaurants tack a menu onto their door for browsers—and will have either an English menu or someone who can translate for you. Even so, sooner or later you'll be rudely surprised as I was when my 'pepperoni' pizza arrived covered with green peppers. Service is normally included although it's customary to round the bill up after a good meal.

For most visitors the rich pastries, the wine and the beer provide the fondest memories of Germany's cuisine. The wine, mostly white, is particularly good from the Mosel, Rhine, Danube, east Austria, and southwest Switzerland areas. Order wine by the 'viertel' or quarter litre. You can say 'Ein viertel suss' (sweet), 'halbe trochen' (medium) or 'trochen' (dry) 'weiss' (white) or 'rot' (red) 'wein' (wine) 'bitte' (please).

The Germans enjoy a tremendous variety of great beer. The average German, who drinks forty gallons of beer a year, knows that 'dunkel' is dark, 'hell' is light, 'flaschenbier' is bottled and 'vom fass' is on tap. 'Pils normales' is barley-based, 'weize' is wheat based and 'malzbier' is the malt beer that children learn on. When you order beer, ask for 'ein halb' for a half litre or 'ein mass' for a whole litre. Some beerhalls only serve it by the litre.

ACCOMMODATION

While accommodation in Germany, Switzerland, and Austria is fairly expensive it is normally very comfortable and good value. Plan on spending £20 per double in big cities, £11.50 in towns.

I have assumed you'll be needing doubles and the prices listed are for doubles (including breakfast). The more people you put in a hotel room, the cheaper it gets. While hotel singles are most expensive, private accommodation (zimmers) have a flat per person rate. Hostels and dormitories always charge per person. People staying several nights are most desirable. One night stays are sometimes given an extra charge.

The listings in this book are places that I have slept in or reviewed recently. In recommending a hotel I like places that are in a convenient, central, quiet and safe location, small, family-run with local character, simple facilities not catering to foreign 'needs', inexpensive, friendly, English-speaking, and clean. Obviously a friendly, clean, quiet, central, cheap room is virtually impossible to find and all of my recommendations fall short of perfection—sometimes miserably. But I've listed the best values for each price category that I could find, given the above criteria.

While you'll see lots of 'no vacancy' signs in July, August and during a few scattered holiday periods, reservations are not normally necessary. During peak times, or if you want a particular place, call ahead or try to arrive early. I've taken great pains to list telehone numbers with long distance instructions. Use the telephone. A hotel receptionist will trust you, holding a room until 5pm. Please don't let these people down. If you say you'll come, come. Or call and cancel.

Accommodation categories in descending order of price are: Hotel, Hotel Garni (room and breakfast only, no other meals), Pension, Gasthof, Fremdenzimmer, Zimmer frei (private home), Youth hostel, camping, and park bench. Room lists are always available at local tourist offices and remaining vacancies are often posted there after hours. Normally the cost of a room includes a continental breakfast, taxes, service and showers either in the room or down the hall. This price is usually posted in the room. Before accepting confirm that breakfast is included. The only tip the hotels I've listed would like is a friendly, easy-going guest.

Those camping should get a camping guide for the area. You'll find camp sites just about wherever you need them. Look for 'Campingplatz' signs. Camping is a popular middle-class family way to go among Germans. You'll find that camp sites are cheap, friendly, safe and very rarely full.

Youth hostellers can take advantage of the wonderful network of hostels (see listing later). Follow the signs marked 'Jugendherberge'. Triangles and the 'tree next to a house' are also youth hostel symbols. Generally you must have a membership card (check with your local YHA for details of international membership), though sometimes non-members are admitted for an extra charge.

Hostels are open to members of all ages (except in Bavaria where a 26 year maximum age is strictly enforced). They usually cost £2.25–£4.50 per night (plus sheet hire if you don't have your own), and serve good cheap meals or provide kitchen facilities. While many have couple or family rooms, plan on beds in segregated dormitories—five to twenty per room. Hostels can be idyllic and peaceful, or school groups can raise the rafters. I like small hostels best.

YOUTH HOSTELS—JUDENDHERBERGE

Listed below are the youth hostels that fall within easy striking distance of our tour. They are grouped in regions with each hostel's address, phone number, and number of beds listed. For a complete listing of Europe's 2,000 hostels pick up an international directory at any hostel.

Romantic Road region

Frankfurt—Haus der Jugend, Deutschherrunfer 12, 6000 Frankfurt/Main 70, tel 0611/619058, 500 beds.

Wurzburg—Burkarderstr. 44, 8700 Wurzburg, tel 0931/ 705913, 150 beds.

Igersheim—Erlenbachtalstr. 44, 6991 Igersheim/b. Bad Mergentheim, tel 07931/6373, 150 beds.

Creglingen—Erdbacherstr. 30, 6993 Creglingen, tel 07933/336, 114 beds.

Weikershrim—Haus der Musik, Im heiligen Wohr, 6992 Weikersheim, tel 07934/7025, 110 beds.

Rothenburg—1) Rossmuhle 8803 Rothenburg/Tauber, tel 0986/510, 141 beds.

2) Spitalhof, Postfach 1206, 8803 Rothenburg/Tauber, tel 09861/4510, 141 beds.

Feuchtwangen—Dr. Guthlein-Weg 1, 8805 Feuchtwangen, tel 09852/842, 152 beds.

Dinkelsbuhl—Koppengasse 10, 8804 Dinkelsbuhl, tel 09851/509, 150 beds.

Rechenberg—Schloss, Zum Schloss 7, 7181 Stimpfach-Rechtenberg, tel 07967/372, 116 beds.

Nordlingen—Kaiserwiese 1, 8860 Nordlingen, tel 09081/84109, 80 beds.
Donauworth—Goethestr. 10, 8850 Donauworth, tel 0906/5158, 130 beds.
Munich—1) Wendl-Dietrich Str. 20, 8000 Munchen 19, tel 089/1311560, 510 beds.

  2) Jugendgasthaus, Miesingstr. 4, 8000 Munchen 70, tel 089/7236550, 344 beds.
Pullach (near Munich)—Burg Schwaneck, Burgweg 4–6, 8023 Pullach, tel 089/7932381, 130 beds.

Bavaria—Tyrolia

Reutte—6600 Reutte, Prof Dengel-Strasse 20, Tirol, tel 05672/3039, 28 beds.
Reutte-Hofen—6600 Reutte, Jugendgasthaus am Graben, Postfach 3, Tirol, tel 05672/2644, 860, 38 beds.
Fussen—Mariahilferstr. 5, 8958 Fussen (Allgau), tel 08362/7754, 150 beds.
Oberammergau—Malensteinweg 10, 8103 Oberammergau, tel 08822/4114, 130 beds.
Garmisch-Partenkirchen—Jochstr. 10, 8100 Garmisch-Partenkirchen, tel 0882/2980, 290 beds.
Mittenwald—Buckelwiesen 7, 8102 Mittenwald, tel 08823/1701, 140 beds.
Innsbruck—1) 6020 Innsbruck, Reichenauerstr. 147, Tirol, tel 05222/46179, 190 beds.

  2) Studentenheim, 6020 Innsbruck, Reichenauerstr. 147, tel 05222/46179, 112 beds.

  3) 6020 Innsbruck, Rennweg 176, Tirol, tel 05222/25814, 100 beds.

  4) 6020 Innsbruck, Sillg 8a, Tirol, tel 05222/31311, 100 beds.

  5) 6020 Innsbruck, Volkshaus, Radetzkystr. 47, tel 05222/46684, 52 beds.
Salzburg/Salzkammergut—1) 5026 Salzburg, Aigner Strasse 34, tel 0662/23248, 19 beds.

  2) 5020 Salzburg-Nonntal, Josef-Preis Allee 18, tel 0662/42670, 360 beds.

  3) Eduard-Heinrich-Haus, 5020 Salzburg-Josefau, Eduard-Heinrich-Str. 2, tel 0662/25976, 153 beds.

  4) 5020 Salzburg, Glockengasse 8, tel 0662/76241, 152 beds.

  5) 5020 Salzburg, Hannspergstrasse 27, tel 0662/75030, 108 beds.

  6) 5020 Salzburg, HausderJugend, Franz Hinterholzer Kai 8, 70 beds.
St Gilgen—5340 St Gilgen, Haus Schafbergblick, Mond Seerstr. 7–11, Salzburg, 1 tel 06227/365, 70 beds.

Bad Ischl—4820 Bad Ischl, Am Rechensteg 5, Oberosterreich, tel 06132/2577, 140 beds.
Hallstatt-Lahn—4830 Hallstatt-Lahn 50, Oberosterreich, tel 06134/279, 53 beds.
Gosau—4824 Gosau, Dr Eder-Haus, Oberosterreich, tel 06136/352, 68 beds.
Obertraun—4831 Obertraun, Winkl 26, Oberosterreich, tel 06134/360, 160 beds.
Bad Aussee—8990 Bad Aussee, Lerchenreith 148, Steiermark, tel 06152/2238, 156 beds.

Vienna/Danube

Vienna—1) Jugendgasthaus Wein-Brigittenau, 1200 Wien, Friedrich Engelsplatz 24, tel 0222/338294, 258 beds.
   2) 1070 Wien, Myrthengasse 7, tel 0222/936316, 123 beds.
   3) 1030 Wien III, Lechnerstrasse 12, tel 0222/731494, 52 beds.
   4) Ruthensteiner JH, 1150 Wien XV, Robert Hamerlinggase 24, tel. 0222/834693, 77 beds.
   5) 1130 Wien XIII, Jugendherberge der Stadt Wien (Hutteldorf), Schlossberggasse 8, tel 0222/821501, 273 beds.
Melk—3390 Melk an der Donau, Abt-Karl-Strasse 42, Niederosterreich, tel 02752/2681, 66 beds.

Appenzell

Appenzell—Schwende-Weissbad, 9057 Weissbad, tel 071/881189, 35 beds.
St Gallen—Juchstrasse 25/ Speicherstrasse, 9000 St Gallen, tel 071/243444, 142 beds.
Wildhaus—Unterwasser-Befang, 9658 Wildhaus (St Gallen), tel 074/51270, 75 beds.
Schaan—Vaduz-untere Ruttigasse 6, 9494 Schaan-Vaduz, tel 075/25022, 104 beds.

Interlaken/Jungfrau Region

Interlaken—Bonigen—Aareweg 21, as See, 3806 Bonigen (Bern), tel 036/224353, 200 beds.
Gimmelwald—Beim Rest Schilthorn, 3801 Gimmelwald (Bern), tel 036/551704, 44 beds.
Grindelwald—Terrassenweg, 3818 Grindelwald (Bern), tel 036/531009, 133 beds.
Brienz—Strandweg 10, am See, 3855 Brienz (Bern), tel 036/511152, 100 beds.

Southwest Switzerland

Zweisimmen—3770 Zweisimmen-Tull (Bern), tel 030/22188, 130 beds.

Saanen—Chalet Rublihorn, 3792 Saanen, tel 030/41343, 40 beds.
Chateau d'Oex—Les Riavx, 1837 Chateau d'Oex (Vaud), tel
029/46404, 52 beds.
Montreux—Haut Lac, Passage de l'auberge 8, 1820 Territet
(Vaud), tel 021/634934, 114 beds.
Lausanne—Chemin du Muguet 1, 1007 Lausanne-ouchy (Vaud),
tel 021/265782, 180 beds.

West Switzerland
Bern—Jugendhaus, Weihergasse 4, 3005 Bern, tel 031/226316,
144 beds.
Avenches—rue du Lavoir 5, 1580 Avenches (Vaud), tel
037/752666, 78 beds.
Biel—Solothurnerstrasse 137, 2504 Biel (Bern), tel 032/412965,
40 beds.
Neuchatel—rue du Suchiez 35, 2006 Neuchatel, tel 038/257940,
66 beds.

Black Forest
Lorrach—Steinenweg 40, 7850 Lorrach, tel 0762/7040, 163 beds.
Kandern-Platzhof—Auf der Scheideck, 7853 Steinen
(Schwarzwald), tel 07626/484, 74 beds.
Wieden—JH Belchen, Oberwieden 16, Am Wiedener Eck 7861
Wieden, tel 07673/538, 176 beds.
Todtnauberg—Fleinerhaus, Radscherstr 12, 7868 Todtnau 2, tel
07671/275, 156 beds.
Feldberg—Hebelhof Passhohe 14, 7821 Feldberg (Schwarzwald),
tel 07676/221, 260 beds.
Freiberg—Kartauserstr 151, 7800 Freiburg, tel 0761/67656, 375
beds.
Breisach—Munsterbergstr 30 – 33, 7814 Breisach (Schwarzwald),
tel 07667/7665, 88 beds.
Baden-Baden—Hardberstr 34, 7570 Baden-Baden, tel
07221/52223, 144 beds.

Mosel
Trier—Maarstr 156, 5500 Trier/Mosel, tel 0651/41092, 312 beds.
Bernkastel-Kues—Jugendherbergsstr. 1,5550 Bernkastel-
Kues/Mosel, tel 06531/2395, 140 beds.
Traven-Trarbach—Am Hirtenpfadchen, 5580 Traven-Trarbach,
tel 06541/9278, 190 beds.
Cochem—Klottenerstr 9, 5590 Cochem/Mosel, tel 02671/8633,
177 beds.
Brodenbach—Moorkamp 7, 5401 Brodenbach/Mosel, tel
02605/3389, 137 beds.

Rhine

Koln—1) Koln-Riehl, Jugendgasthaus, An der Schanze 14 5000 Koln 60, tel 0221/767081, 366 beds.
2) Koln-Deutz, Siegesstr 5a, 5000 Koln, 21, tel 0221/814/711, 364 beds.
Bonn—Venusberg, Haager Weg 42, 5300 Bonn 1 (Rheinland), tel 0228/281200, 276 beds.
Bonn-Bad Godesberg—Jugendgasthaus, Horionstr. 60, 5300 Bonn 2 (Rheinland), tel 0228/317516, 90 beds.
St Goar—Bismarckweg 17, 5401 St Goar, tel 06741/388, 160 beds.
Oberwesel—Jugendgasthaus, Auf dem Schonberg, 6532 Oberwesel, tel 06744/8355, 102 beds.
Bacharach—Jugendburg Stahleck, 6533 Bacharach/Rhein, tel 06743/1266, 207 beds.
Bingen-Bingerbruck—Herter Str 51, 6530 Bingen 1, Bingerbruck/Rhein, tel 06721/32163, 194 beds.

COMMUNICATING IN GERMAN

All but two days of this tour are in German-speaking areas. While you'll hear lots of English in touristed areas, train stations, hotels and in the tourist offices, and you can manage on this trip speaking only English, a little understanding of German will give your trip a real bonus.

I carried a small dictionary in the glove compartment and a German Phrase Book with me most of the time. I also enjoyed a routine of learning (and using) five new words a day. Here are a few tips for the lazy linguist and a list of words I found most useful. When you're in a bind remember the Swiss in general and young people everywhere are most likely to understand your English *if* you keep it clean, simple and pronounce every letter.

The Germans have a couple of twists to their way of writing and pronouncing. 'W' is always pronounced like a 'v', and 'i' usually sounds like a long 'e'. 'J' is like 'y', 'ch' like the 'ch' in the Scottish 'loch', 'r's' are rolled, 'sch' like 'sh', 'tsch' like 'ch', 'tz' and 'z' like 'ts' in 'sits'. They have a letter which looks like our cursive capital 'b' and is pronounced like a double 'S'. Two dots over vowels is an umlaut. These have sounds rare in English. To make an umlaut sound you make your lips round to say 'o' but try to say 'e'. (Out of pure laziness, I've left the umlauts out of this book, sorry.)

An understanding of how English (which is a 'Germanic' language), German and Latin relate is very helpful. For instance, English words ending in 'ic' are usually Latin. To make that word German, replace the 'ic' with 'ish' (barbaric—barbarish, fantastic—fantastish, esoteric—esoterish). Won't it be fun to be able to say 'comic' and 'idiotic' on your trip? Also 'ise' English words become 'izerin' words auf Deutsch (vocalise—vocalizerin, economise—economizerin).

Germany has some fun combination words. Be on the lookout for words like 'Fingerhut'—finger house (thimble), 'Halbinsel'—half island (peninsula), and 'Stinktier'—stinky animal (skunk).

Each country has a distinct dialect which is difficult for us to hear. The Swiss speak Swiss-German but write High-German like the Germans. They'll greet you with a cherry 'Greutzi', say goodbye with a 'Ciao' (pron. Jo), and use 'Merci' for thank you. Austrians speak a lilting dialect close to Bavarian. People in both regions greet each other with 'Gruss Gott' (May God greet you).

GERMAN VOCABULARY FOR TRAVELLERS

Hello guten tag
How are you? Wie geht es?
I'm fine, thanks. Es geht mir gut, danke.
Please bitte
Thank you danke schon
See you later bis bald
Goodnight gute nacht
Goodbye auf wiedersehn
Yes/no ja/nein
Good/bad gut/schlecht
Beautiful/ugly schon/hasslich
Big/small gross/klein
Fast/slow schnell/langsam
Very sehr
Enough genug
How much? Wieviel?
Money geld
Cheap/expensive billig/teuer
Complete price (everything included) alles ist inbegriffen
I don't understand. Ich verstehe nicht.
What do you call this? Wie heisst das?
I'm tired. Ich bin mude.
I ich
You du
Love liebe
Sleep schlaf
Friend freund
Castle schloss
Valley tal
Train zug
Station bahnhof
Toilet klo
Tourist Information verkehrsamt (or) i
Post and telephone office PTT
What time is it? Wieviel uhr ist es?
Yesterday gestern
Today heute
Tomorrow morgen
This evening heute abend
Morning morgen
Rest day ruhetag
Vacation urlaub
Where is...? Wo ist...?

To the right rechts
To the left links
I'm lost. Ich habe mich verirrt.
I am rich and single Ich bin reich und einzel.
I am rich and single? Ich bin reich und einzel.
Room for rent zimmer (or) zimmerfrei (or) fremdenzimmer (or)
gastezimmer
Double bed room doppelbett zimmer
Single room einselbett zimmer
Dormitory schlafsaal (or) lager (or) massen lager (or)
matratzenlager
Without shower (with) ohne dusche (mit)
Holiday apartments (long term only, 5 day minimum)
ferienwohnung
No vacancy belegt
Adult erwachsen
Petrol—regular benzin (2 star)
Petrol—unleaded bleifrei
Petrol—super super (4 star)
Diesel diesel
Self-service ("sb" at petrol stations) selbstbedienung
Guided tour fuhrung

Numbers
Zero null
One eins
Two zwei
Three drei
Four vier
Five funf
Six sechs
Seven sieben
Eight acht
Nine neun
Ten zehn
Eleven elf
Twelve zwolf
Thirteen dreizehn
Fourteen vierzehn
Fifteen funfzehn
Sixteen sechzehn
Seventeen siebzehn
Eighteen achtzehn
Nineteen neunzehn
Twenty zwanzig
Twenty-one einundzwanzig

Twenty-two zweiundzwanzig
Twenty-three dreiundzwanzig
Twenty-four vierundzwanzig
Twenty-five funfundzwanzig
Thirty dreissig
Thirty-five funfunddreissig
Thirty-six sechsunddreissig
Thirty-seven siebenunddreissig
Thirty-eight achtunddreissig
Thirty-nine neununddreissig
Forty vierzig
Fifty funfzig
Sixty sechzig
Seventy siebzig
Eighty achtzig
Ninety neunzig
One hundred hundert
One hundred twenty-five hundertfunfundzwanzig
One hundred fifty hundertfunfzig
One hundred seventy-five hundertfunfundsiebzig
Two hundred zweihundert
Two hundred fifty zweihundertfunfzig
Three hundred dreihundert
Four hundred vierhundert
Five hundred funfhundert
Seven hundred siebenhundert
One thousand tausend
One thousand one hundred tausendeinhundert
Two thousand zweitausend
Five thousand funftausend
Ten thousand zehntausend

Food vocabulary
Food speise
Grocery shop supermarkt
Picnic picknick
Delicious lecker
Market markt
Drunk betrunken
Cheers! prosit!
I'm hungry. Ich habe hunger.
Water wasser
Coffee kaffee
Tea tee
Milk milch
Beer bier

Wine wein
Cider obstwein
Lemonade zitronensaft
Hors d'oeuvres vorspeise
Bread brot
Soup suppe
Eggs eier
Fish fisch
Lobster hummer
Meat fleisch
Beef rindfleisch
Beefsteak beefsteak
Pork schweinefleisch
Ham schinken
Mutton hammelfleisch
Veal kalbfleisch
Chicken huhn
Rice reis
Potatoes kartoffeln
Vegetables gemuse
Salad salat
Tomatoes tomaten
Cabbage kohl
Green peas grune erbsen
Beans bohnen
Mushrooms champignons
Cheese kase
Fruit fruchte
Pastries feines geback
Ice cream eis
Biscuits kekse
Orange orange
Apple apfel
Banana banane
Grapes weintraube
Pear birne
Cherries kirschen
Strawberries erdbeeren
Sugar zucker
Cream sahne
Salt salz
Pepper pfeffer
Oil ol
Vinegar essig
Mustard senf
Butter butter

Jam konfiture
Knife messer
Fork gable
Spoon loffel
Bottle flasche
Glass glas
Cup tasse
Plate teller
Napkin serviette
Rare blutig
Medium halbengleich
Well done durch
Warm warm
Cold, iced geeist
Show me the menu. Zeigen sie mir das menu.
I would like... ich mochte...
How much is the meal? Was kostet die mahlzeit?
Is service included? Ist die bedienung inbegriffen?
The bill, please. Die rechnung, bitte.
Breakfast fruhstuck
Lunch mittagessen
Dinner abendessen
To drink trinken
To eat essen

Place names
Many people are confused by German place names that differ
from what we call them in English. Learn these:

West Germany Deutschland, or Bundesrepublik
  Deutschland (BRD)
Romantic Road Romantische Strasse
Munich Munchen
Bavaria Bayern
Bavarian Bayerisch
Black Forest Schwarzwald
Cologne Koln
East Germany Deutsche Demokratische Republik (DDR)
Austria Osterreich
Vienna Wien
Danube Donau
Switzerland Schweiz
Lake Constance Bodensee
Lake Geneva Lac Leman
Lake Lucerne Lac Luzern

TELEPHONING

Too many timid tourists never use the phones. They work and are essential to smart travel. Call hotels in advance to make a reservation whenever you know when you'll be in town. If there's a language problem, ask someone at your hotel to talk to your next hotel for you.

Public phone booths are much cheaper than using the more convenient hotel phones. The key to dialling direct is understanding area codes. For calls to other European countries, dial the international access code (00 in Germany, 00 in Switzerland, and 050 in Austria) followed by the country code, followed by the area code without its zero, and finally the local number (4 to 7 digits). When dialling long distance within a country start with the area code (including its zero) then the local number.

Telephoning the UK from a pay phone is easy. Gather a pile of large coins and find a booth that says international. The best budget approach is to call with a coin and have that person return your call at a specified time at your hotel. From the UK they'd dial 010-country code-area code without zero-local number. Reversed charges, person to person, credit card calls etc. are more expensive and complicated.

City	Area Code	Tourist Info
Frankfurt	0611	231055
Rothenburg	09861	2038
Munich	089	239-1259
Reutte	05672	2336
Salzburg	0662	71712
Hallstatt	06134	208
Vienna	0222	431608
Innsbruck	05222	25715
Hall in Tyrol	05223	6269
Appenzell	071	874111
Interlaken	036	222121
Gimmelwald	036	551955
Montreux	021	631212
Murten	037	715112
Bern	031	227676
Staufen	07633	80536
Baden Baden	07221	275200
Bonn	0228	773466
St Goar	06741	383
Bacharach	06743	1266
Berlin	030	262-6031

Country codes
USA—1
Canada—1
France—33
Belgium—32
West Germany—49
East Germany—37
Italy—39
Netherlands—31
Switzerland—41
Austria—43
Great Britain—44

International code to call out of:
Germany—00
Austria—050
Switzerland—00

Train Info
Munich—592991
Vienna—7200
Bern—222404
St Goar—424

Directory assistance
Germany
    Info, local—118 or 0118
    International assistance—00118

Switzerland
    International directory assistance—191
    T.I.—120
    Weather—162
    Local directory assistance—111

Austria—Vienna
    Info, local—15

International assistance—08

MONEY

Germany—Deutschmarks (DM) are divided into 100 pfennig (pf or p). You'll find 5 pf, 10 pf, 50 pf, 1, 2, and 5 DM coins. Notes come in 10, 20, 50, 100 and 500 denominations.

Austria—Austrian schilling (AS) are divided into 100 groschen. You'll rarely deal with groschen and shillings come in coins of 1, 5, 10 and 20, notes in 20, 50, 100, 500 and 1000 denominations.

Switzerland—The Swiss franc (SF) is divided into 100 centimes. You'll find 10 and 20 cent coins along with ½, 1, 2 and 5 SF coins, 10, 20, 50, 100, 500 and 1000 SF notes. The ½ franc coin is often confused with the smaller coins. Notice the ½ franc is the one with ridges on its edge.